Clicking With Clients: Online Marketing For Private Practice Therapists

By Daniel Wendler, M.A.

Contents

Introduction

It's easy to market yourself online as a therapist.

Or at least, it should be.

That's why I wrote this book. Online marketing seems complicated but it's easier than it looks. If you were able to make it through your graduate training, you're smart enough to learn how to attract new clients online.

How can I be so sure? Well, I know quite a bit about both marketing and therapy.

My Story

My name is Daniel Wendler (nice to meet you!). I'm a graduate student in clinical psychology and plan to have a long career as a therapist.

Before starting my career in mental health, I worked for several years as an online marketer. I helped large clients such as PGA Tour Superstore and Dog.com grow their digital sales, and was mentored by some of the brightest minds in the marketing industry. I also launched a few online businesses of my own, including ImproveYourSocialSkills.com and MarketingforTherapists.org. I'm no internet millionaire, but I know a thing or two about success in the online world.

I wrote this book because I wanted to share my knowledge of online marketing with my fellow therapists. Whether you're a counselor, a psychologist, or any other mental health specialist, I hope you'll find this guide helpful. Pull up a chair (or a couch, if you've got a psychoanalytic bent) and let's get started.

The Guide

Marketing For Therapists is divided into seven sections.

- **Launch Your Site** explains how to get online.

- **Design Your Site** walks you through the visual design of your website.

- **Get New Clients** explains strategies for attracting new clients on Google, therapist directions, and social media.

- **Protect Your Privacy** teaches you how to keep clients from discovering personal information about you online.

- **Self-Publishing Success** provides you with a step-by-step guide to marketing your practice through a self-published book.

- **Profitable Online Advertising** gives you a crash-course in the world of online advertising, complete with strategies for maximizing your advertising results.

- **Recommended Resources** is a list of helpful links, professionals, and tools.

I start with simple topics like choosing a web host, and move into more complex topics like SEO and advertising. If the earlier content feels a bit too basic for you, feel free to jump ahead.

Recommendation Links

Throughout the guide, I'll be recommending a variety of online resources that can help with your private practice.

I chose these resources because I believe in them. I've used most of these recommendations myself and can personally vouch for them. In the rare occasion where I haven't used a recommendation personally, I chose it after doing extensive research.

For full disclosure, I want to let you know that some companies that I recommend pay rewards whenever someone refers a new client to them. Customers don't pay anything extra – the company just pays a finder's fee as a thanks for the referral. I don't choose companies to recommend based on their rewards, but I do sign up for the referral program if I was going to recommend a company anyway.

In order to get credit for referring the people who read this book, I've created some links which pass through my website and go straight to the site I recommend. For instance, if you type in MarketingForTherapists.org/BrighterVision, you will be taken to BrighterVision.com and Brighter Vision will give me credit for referring you.

This extra income is a big help to me, and there is no downside to you using these referral links. But if you'd prefer not to give me credit for your sign up, just use Google to search for the website I recommend and go there directly.

Why Online Marketing?

Online marketing can feel overwhelming.

There are a thousand different strategies that you can pursue. Do you start a blog? Build your Twitter followers? See if anyone is still on Myspace?

After you choose a strategy, you have to deal with the steep learning curve. If you start a blog, how do you get people to read it? If you pay for a new website, how do you make sure you get your money's worth? Graduate school prepared you to work with clients, but actually finding those clients is a whole other story!

Given these challenges, it's understandable that some therapists prefer to ignore online marketing entirely. But many clients start their search for a therapist online, and even word-of-mouth clients. Unless you have an ironclad source of referrals, online marketing isn't optional.

If the last paragraph increased your blood pressure, you're not alone. Many of the therapists I work with tell me things like, "I hate marketing!" or, "Why can't I spend all my time with clients?" If you're not sure what to do, it's easy for online marketing to stress you out.

But if you know what you're doing, online marketing can actually be pretty awesome.

It gives you the opportunity to be creative in a new way. If you've ever wanted to be a writer or a designer, you'll enjoy writing your blog and customizing the look of your website.

It helps you meet your financial goals. Online marketing is one of the best ways to bring in new clients and improve your bottom line. One day, you might even use your marketing skills to produce passive income through an ebook or an online course.

And, online marketing can be fun! I feel great when someone comments on my blog or my website traffic reaches a new record. Even if you don't think of yourself as a marketing person, you might end up enjoying yourself – as long as you take the time to learn the fundamentals first.

So my hope is that after finishing this book, you won't view online marketing as a chore or a stressor. Instead, you'll see it as an opportunity – an opportunity to grow your practice, reach your financial goals, and maybe have a little fun along the way.

Ready? Let's get started.

Launch Your Therapy Site

If you want to market yourself online, you need a website. A website allows you to share information about your practice, attract new clients, and provide an easy way for people to sign up for therapy.

In order to get a website, you need three ingredients.

1. **A Domain Name** – This allows people to find your website. Think of this like the street address of a new house.

2. **A Web Host.** A web host runs the servers that your site will live on. Think of this like the plot of land that you will build a house on.

3. **Software to Build Your Website.** The tools you will use to create your website. Think of this like the construction crew that builds your house.

In this section, I'll show you how to choose each of these three ingredients. I'll also explain how to get a professional email address. Let's dive in!

Domain Names for Therapists

The first step in marketing your practice online is getting a domain name.

A domain name is your address on the web. Just as people need your home address to visit you, people need a domain name to get to your website. For instance, MarketingForTherapists.org is the domain name of my website. When you type it into your web browser, your browser knows how to get you to my site.

A domain name is also part of your brand image. For instance, if I had named my website "BecomeATherapistMillionareInstantly.com", it wouldn't have seemed very credible. Or if I named my website "TherapyYeti.com," it wouldn't be clear what I was offering.

The same thing is true for your website. You want a domain name that is 1) relevant to what you offer, and that 2) has a professional feel. Would you want to get counseling from someone who runs Bob-TheTherapyDude.com?

Because many good domain names are already taken, it might take a few tries to find one that is available and that fits your practice. Fortunately, I'm here to help. I'll give you some strategies for finding an available domain name, and then I'll walk you through the steps you need to take to actually register it.

How To Pick A Domain Name

Here are some recommendations for building your domain name. These aren't rigid rules – if you have a great idea that's not listed, go ahead and use that. But if you're not sure what to do, follow one of these formulas:

For A Solo Practice

- YourName (ie, JohnSmith.com)
- YourDegree+YourName (DrJohnSmith.com, JohnSmithLPC.com)
- YourDegree+YourLastName (DrSmith.com, DrSmithPhD.com, SmithMFT.com)
- YourName+YourRole(JohnSmithCounselor.com, JohnSmithTherapist.com)
- YourName+WhatYouOffer (JohnSmithCounseling.com JohnSmithTherapy.com)

For A Specific Focus

- Condition+Treatment (AnxietyCounseling.com, DepressionHope.com)
- Condition + Treatment + Location (PortlandAnxietyCounseling.com)
- Population+Treatment (CounselingForVeterans.com, LGBTCounseling.com)

All-Purpose Formulas

- Location + Treatment (ChicagoTherapy.com, MinnesotaCounselor.com)
- Name of Clinic (AcmeCounselingCenter.com)

Domain Name FAQs

Do I get a .com, .org. .net, or something else?

If you can get a .com with your preferred name, you should. They are the most common domain name endings, so you should use .com if you can.

If the .com of your preferred name is taken, you can try a .net or a .org. Don't do anything other than .com, .org or .net (anything else looks unprofessional and sketchy.) Bear in mind that registering a .net or .org website tends to be more expensive than registering a .com.

Should I get more than one domain name?

Most therapists only need one domain name for their practice. More than that will just increase your domain registration costs and potentially confuse clients.

However, it's not a bad idea to have one domain name for yourself as an individual and another domain name for your private practice.

For instance, you might have DrJohnSmith.com and JohnSmith-CounselingCenter.com. You would use the first domain as an elaborate business card, and the second domain to promote your counseling center.

Should I get the same domain name in both .com and .org?

You should only this if you are concerned someone might try to impersonate your practice online. For instance, if you work with a lot of court-ordered clients, you might want to register common variations of your name to protect against disgruntled clients.

However, every domain you register will cost you $10+ dollars per year. That adds up quickly if you register extra domains. So I recommend you only register multiple domain variations if you have a good reason, or if you feel the peace of mind is worth the extra cost.

I picked out the perfect name but someone already took it! What do I do?

Try to register the domain on .org or .net if it's not available on .com — that's what I did with marketingfortherapists.org.

If it's taken on .org and .net as well, you should probably pick another name. You can either come up with a brand new name, or try to modify your chosen name slightly. For instance, if Your-NameLPC.com is taken, perhaps you could try LPCYourName.com

In some cases it's possible to buy a domain name from the current owner, but this will usually cost you thousands of dollars. If you have that kind of money to burn, go for it, but you are probably better off finding a new name.

How to Register Your Domain Name

It's pretty easy.

First, head to NameCheap.com (or MarketingForTherapists.org/ NameCheap if you don't mind me earning a finder's fee.) I recommend NameCheap because they have good prices and good customer service. You can use another registrar if you prefer, but make sure to check both the first year price and the renewal price. Some registrars (such as Godaddy) lure you in with a cheap price for the first year, and then raise the price when you renew your domain.

Next, type your desired domain into the big ol' box on their home-page. If it's available, add it to your cart. If it's not, try another do-main name until you find one that's available.

After that, all you need to do is check out! You probably don't need any add-ons, so don't worry about SSL, private email, etc. You also don't need to register other versions of your domain. It might be su-per cheap to register YourDomain.biz, but you will probably never use that extra version, so save your money.

Your total cost should be about $10-$15 per year. You can pay for up to ten years at a time. I recommend that you go ahead and register your domain for 10 years — that way you don't have to worry about it for a long time. However, if you're not sure you'll stick with your website, it's okay to register your domain for just a year or two (but make sure you renew!)

How to use your domain name with your website

Once you have your domain name set up and your website hosting secured, you need to point your domain name at your website. Ask Namecheap support for assistance, or look on their help page.

How To Build Your Website

Once you have your domain name set up, it's time to build your website.

Unless you happen to be a skilled programmer, you can't make a website from scratch. Instead, you'll need to use a website design software (or hire someone to do it for you.) I'll explain all your options in this section.

Keep in mind that this section is just about choosing the software you'll use to design your website. My advice on how to design your website is later in the book. So stay tuned!

Wordpress

Wordpress.org

Wordpress is the most affordable option for therapist websites – and the most powerful.

Wordpress is free software, which means you only need to pay for the servers that your website runs on. It's easy to find free guides to teach you how to use Wordpress or free plugins that add new features to your site.

With Wordpress, you can design a feature-packed website without a programmer or web designer. I have built all my website in Wordpress, and I don't know how to code at all.

The downside is that Wordpress takes some time to learn, and requires more technical skill than some of the other options. If you're not very tech-savvy, or if you don't have much time to spend learning a new software, it might not be the best choice. You will also probably need to pay for a premium theme in order to make your website look good (which I discuss later in the guide.)

However, if you are willing to put some time into learning Wordpress and customizing your website, you could find yourself with a beautiful website that didn't cost you very much. And Wordpress skills are highly marketable. You might find yourself making a little extra cash designing websites for other therapists, too!

You can check out Wordpress at Wordpress.org. If you want to use Wordpress, you'll need to pay for a Wordpress web host (discussed in my next section.)

Weebly

MarketingForTherapists.org/Weebly

Like Wordpress, Weebly is a website building software.

Unlike WordPress, you don't need to worry about hosting or any of the technical stuff — Weebly hosts your site on their own servers and they handle all the technical stuff for you.

Weebly makes it super easy to design good-looking websites. It can't do as many things as WordPress, but what it does, it does well. My sister built her website (RachaelWendler.com) on Weebly, and it looks great.

Compared to WordPress, Weebly is easier to learn. It has fewer features, but that might make it easier for you to focus on what's important. If you want as many features and customizability as possible, go with Wordpress. If you want a website that gives you less options but has less of a learning curve, go with Weebly.

The best news? It only costs $8 per month, and you can try it for free. Give them a try at MarketingForTherapists.org/Weebly.

Strikingly

MarketingForTherapists.org/Strikingly

Strikingly is a one-page website builder. People scroll down until they reach the end, no clicking required. NiceCreamFactory.com is a good example of a Strikingly site.

Strikingly's websites are beautiful, mobile friendly, and easy to set up. Best of all, Strikingly's website are, well, striking. They stand out compared to other therapist websites, so if you want a look that will get people's attention, Strikingly is a good choice.

The downside is that Strikingly's websites work best when they're short. If you're planning on having a blog or adding lots of content, Strikingly is probably not a good option for you. However, if you just want to present your basic information, the conditions you treat, and a contact form, Strikingly would work really well. Strikingly is even better if you just want a place to host your online CV.

If you plan to have a short website with limited content, Strikingly is your best bet. Otherwise, Wordpress or Weebly will be a better choice.

Strikingly costs $12 per month, or $8 if you pay for an entire year at once. They also have a free plan, so you can test them out and see if they look good.

Try them out at MarketingForTherapists.org/Strikingly.

Brighter Vision

MarketingForTherapists.org/BrighterVision

Brighter Vision makes custom websites for therapists. You start by picking one of their templates, and their team of designers will customize it to look and feel exactly how you want it. If you decide you want a different design later on, they'll update your look for free.

Brighter Vision offers free & unlimited technical support, which gives you peace of mind in case your website ever breaks. Plus, they work exclusively with therapists, so you're guaranteed a support team that understands your business.

The main downside is the cost ($59 per month). That's significantly more than the other options I mentioned, and it might seem like a lot of money.

But the better your website, the more likely a client is to sign up with you. Paying a little more to get an attractive website seems like a worthwhile cost to me.

And you should consider the time savings as well. Every hour you spend on your website is an hour you're not spending with clients. It might be worth paying Brighter Vision just to free up a few extra hours each month.

Of course, Brighter Vision isn't for everyone. If you feel pretty confident in your web design skills, or if you have a tight budget, you might want to try one of the do-it-yourself options. But if you want an expert to guarantee results, give Brighter Vision a call.

Try Brighter Vision by visiting MarketingForTherapists.org/BrighterVision. Mention my name to get your first month free.

Hire a Freelancer

A service like Brighter Vision is probably the best option for most therapists looking for a professional website. But if you need some special features that they don't provide, or you want a super-premium website, you might consider hiring a freelancer to design a custom site.

Unfortunately, professional web developers are expensive. A good developer will probably charge between $1000 and $4000 to design your website. It's possible to find cheaper web designers, but like anything, you get what you pay for.

In order to find professional developers, I recommend two options. You can ask other therapists who have great websites for recommendations. Or, you can try the "For Hire" forum on Reddit (Reddit.com/r/ForHire). Reddit's For Hire forum is frequented by lots of skilled web developers, and it's a good place to look for help.

When you're considering which developer is right for you, start by looking at their portfolio. A good developer should have designed several websites that you can peruse. Pay attention to the general look and feel of the website, and also the attention to detail. If there are sloppy mistakes in their portfolio, cross them off the list.

You should also feel a good sense of interpersonal connection with your developer. There's no need to be friends, but you should have a sense that you're communicating well and working together effectively. Think of it like a "therapeutic relationship" but for your website.

Finally, you should come to an agreement on what happens after the developer has built your website. Will they continue to host it and manage it (if so, how much will that cost?) If you don't like their design, will they change it for you? Will they teach you how to make basic updates and changes? There's no one right answer to these questions, but it's important for you to discuss them with your developer and come to answers that both of you feel good about.

WordPress Hosting For Therapists

I'm a Wordpress fanboy. It's easy to use once you get the hang of it, and you can make pretty much any site you can imagine.

However, a WordPress site is only as good as the host you choose. Your host runs the servers that power your WordPress website, and if those servers are no good, then your website will load very slowly — or completely crash under heavy traffic!

I've done a lot of research, and I've come up with two of the best hosts out there. I've picked one host that's ideal if you're on a tight budget, and another host that's great if you're willing to spend a little more for blazing speed and bulletproof security.

By the way, only Wordpress requires you to find a host. Other website solutions have hosting included. So you can skip this section if you are going with Weebly or another non-Wordpress option.

Budget: A Small Orange

MarketingForTherapists.org/ASmallOrange

A Small Orange might have a strange name, but they know how to run a webserver. They have 24/7 support, consistently high reviews, and a reputation for happy customers.

Their plans start at just $3 per month, which is probably less than you spend at Starbucks each week. Most people will be fine with their "Tiny" plan, but you can do the "Small" plan if you want more storage space.

If you're on a budget or just starting out, A Small Orange is a good choice. A Small Orange is also a great option if you are wanting to run a non-commercial website, such as a personal blog. Since you won't be making money from a non-commercial website, a low-cost host is ideal.

In summary:

- Extremely affordable
- Great reputation for site performance and customer service
- The right choice if you are budget-conscious

Sign up at MarketingForTherapists.org/ASmallOrange.

Power: WP Engine

MarketingForTherapists.org/WPEngine

WP Engine has a reputation for being blazing fast. They provide WordPress hosting and nothing else, so their servers are totally optimized for WordPress.

Plus, they provide managed hosting, which means that they do all the work to keep your website updated and protected against security threats. This is important because WordPress receives regular patches to protect against hackers and other malicious activity. It's easy to install those patches yourself, but you have to remember to log in to WordPress and launch the updater. WP Engine handles all of that for you, so you don't need to worry about it.

The downside? Their starter plan costs $30/mo. So you're spending about 10 times what you would for A Small Orange.

But you should consider spending the money. Here's why:

Let's say you earn $90 per session. If a faster website brings you a single new client who stays for 4 sessions, you've just earned $360 — and paid for your website for a year. In other words, WP Engine will pay for itself if it attracts one new client each year. I like those odds.

Plus, you want to keep your time focused on running your practice, not keeping your website up to date. That's why WP Engine's management services are so valuable — you don't need to worry about any of the backend stuff.

In summary:

- Relatively expensive
- Blazing fast
- Managed WordPress means they handle the technical stuff for you

Sign up at MarketingForTherapists.org/WPEngine.

WordPress Themes for Therapists

The best part about WordPress is that it's free, incredibly powerful, and not that hard to use.

The bad news about WordPress is that WordPress websites are pretty ugly out of the box. The default WordPress theme is fine if you want a minimal blog, but it won't win you any points for design. Since your therapy website should be designed to attract clients, you want it to look as good as it can.

So how do you make WordPress look better? The answer is themes.

Think of your website as a car. If Wordpress is the engine, then the theme is the car paint job. WordPress software powers your website, but your theme determines how your website looks.

There are thousands of WordPress themes available. You could spend hours browsing through all of the free themes, or looking through the dozens of companies that sell premium themes. And who knows — maybe you'll find an amazing theme, and maybe it will even be free. But honestly, I recommend you skip the search and save yourself a big headache.

For your therapy site, I recommend you pick between two WordPress themes — X Theme and MentalPress. They both cost about $60; they're both modern, beautiful and easy to customize; and they both provide excellent customer service.

X Theme

MarketingForTherapists.org/XTheme

X Theme is the theme that I used to power all my own websites (MarketingForTherapists.org, ImproveYourSocialSkills.com, and DanielWendler.com)

It's easy to customize, has a ton of powerful add-ons, and doesn't require any technical knowledge. Plus, the X Theme support team is super helpful and speedy in their responses. It's not designed specifically as a therapist theme, but it doesn't need to be. It has many versatile customization options, and will allow you to make a great private practice website.

The downside of this theme is that because there are so many customization options, you might find it a bit overwhelming. But you don't need to use all of the customization options. Even straight "out of the box" X looks great. My website DanielWendler.com uses the X theme with very little customization, and I think it looks awesome (if I do say so myself.)

Bottom line: You can't go wrong with the X theme. Sign up at MarketingForTherapists.org/XTheme.

MentalPress

MarketingForTherapists.org/MentalPress

MentalPress is a theme designed specifically for therapists. Much like the X theme, it has a lot of bonus features and it's designed to be easy to customize. I haven't used it myself, but I researched it extensively, and it looks like an excellent choice.

The downside of this theme is that, because it's designed specifically for therapists, you might find it less customizable than the X theme. If you have a very specific idea in mind of how you want your website to look, MentalPress might not be able to help you. But honestly, MentalPress looks great and should work for most therapists.

Bottom line: If you're looking for a quality theme designed specifically for therapists, and you don't mind giving up some customization options, MentalPress is a great choice. Check it out at MarketingForTherapists.org/MentalPress.

Setting Up a Professional Email

Your email address is a crucial part of your online marketing efforts. If your email address is professional, you will appear polished and trustworthy. If not....well, then you seem unpolished and untrustworthy.

This is less of a factor if your clients are older. But if you are treating teens or young adults, you better believe they'll pay attention to your email address.

One option is to pick a free email address that still looks professional. YourNameCounseling@gmail.com is a good option, as is TheNameOfYourPractice@gmail.com. Gmail is usually your best bet for free email, although Hotmail is okay too.

Unfortunately, even if you snag a great free email, there's still a big problem – only paid email has the features that you need as a therapist.

See, only paid email accounts allow you to use your own domain name in your email address, and only paid email accounts allow you to stay HIPAA-compliant. Instead of being YourName@gmail.com, you can use YourName@YourDomain.com. And instead of risking a HIPAA violation, you stay secure.

Here are two other reasons why paid email providers are worth the cost.

Reason 1: Appear More Legitimate

Let's say you're traveling in a foreign city and looking for a place to eat. Would you rather buy dinner from the shady-looking food stand, or the restaurant with a permanent location and uniformed staff?

If you're adventurous, maybe you'd prefer the food stand. But you'd probably agree that your chances of food poisoning are much lower at the fancy restaurant.

Anyone can set up a food stand in a few minutes, so there is no guarantee of quality. But a restaurant that has invested lots of money in a permanent building has a lot to lose if it fails a health check. So you can probably assume that the permanent restaurant has invested more in their quality controls and is a safer place to eat.

Similarly, anyone can register a free email account in seconds. But having a custom email address on your own domain takes time and money. When you invest in a custom email address, you're showing clients you are the real deal. You're showing them that you're committed to your practice, and you're willing to go the extra mile for quality. In short, a professional email address signifies that you are a professional.

Of course, most clients won't consciously choose a therapist based on their email address. But every piece of your marketing – your website, your logo, your email address, etc – influences the way you appear to potential clients. While your email address is unlikely to consciously sway a client, it contributes to their overall impression of you. The more positive their impression of you, the more likely they are to book a session with you.

I understand if you feel reluctant to pay for email when you can get it for free. But think of it this way. Google Apps costs $60 per year, which is about what most clinicians earn from a single therapy session. If a professional email address helps you get one extra session per year, it pays for itself. To me, that seems like a safe bet.

Reason 2: Protect Yourself from the Wrath of HIPAA

I am not a lawyer or a HIPAA expert, and this is not legal advice. Consult with a legal expert to make sure you are in compliance with HIPAA.

However, my (non-expert) understanding is that free email providers are not HIPAA compliant. If you have confidential patient records in your inbox, you could be on the hook for a security breach.

Fortunately, the paid email providers that I recommend will sign a Business Associate Agreement with you, which means that they are a HIPAA-compliant option. You will still need to take some common-sense precautions to ensure that you are HIPAA-compliant (a BAA won't save you if you leave your practice's email open on a public computer, for instance.) But assuming you take the appropriate pre-cautions, a paid email account will provide some extra protection against a HIPAA violation.

Custom Email Providers

There are a lot of HIPAA-compliant email providers out there, but you really only need to consider two. These two are the most well-known, which means they're almost certain to stick around for the long term.

Google Apps

First, there's Google Apps. Google Apps is the best option for a lot of people, because it lets you keep using all the Google services you're used to (Gmail, Google Calendar, etc) with your custom domain. So there's no need for you to learn a new system.

It's also pretty affordable – it costs $5 per user per month, or $60 per year. You can add new users whenever you want, so if you add an-other clinical to your practice it's simple to give them a secure email address.

You can sign up for a free trial of Google Apps by visiting Marketing-ForTherapists.org/GoogleApps.

Hushmail

If you want more security than Google Apps can offer, then you prob-ably want Hushmail.

Like Google Apps, Hushmail is HIPAA-compliant and allows to you use your own domain name. Unlike Google Apps, Hushmail allows you to send encrypted emails that only the client can open – even if someone else is in their inbox.

For instance, let's say a client requests a copy of their session notes. You could send that via normal email, but then you run the risk of someone else opening the email and reading the notes. This isn't likely to happen, but if it did happen it could be catastrophic (imagine a client's spouse learning about an affair or an addiction through your session notes.)

Hushmail solves the problem by letting you ask a question that only the client could answer. For instance, you might ask a client, "When was our last appointment?" or you might agree on a pre-arranged question and answer. In order to open the email, the client must supply the correct answer. If someone else is snooping in the client's inbox, your client's confidential information is protected.

The downside is that Hushmail is $10 per user per month, and it doesn't include all the nifty extras of Google Apps. For many people, Google Apps is probably the better choice. But if you work in a more sensitive area of therapy (such as addiction treatment), or if you just want the highest level of security, then Hushmail may be a wise investment.

You can sign up for Hushmail at MarketingForTherapists.org/GetHushMail.

Already Have an Email Address?

This advice is easy to follow if you are starting your therapy practice from scratch. But what if you've been using a free email address for years?

Well, you could always just keep on using it. Getting a custom email address is nice, but it probably won't make or break your practice.

But if you'd like to switch, there's a pretty easy way to do that. First, update your website so all new clients see your new email address. Then set up your old email address to automatically forward all incoming emails to your new email address. (This sounds complicated but it's not – just search for "automatically forward emails + [your email provider]" and you'll find some guides.)

Once you've done this, then emails to your old address will automatically arrive in your new inbox. You can then reply and let the other person know that you've updated your email. After a month or two, almost everyone should have switched over to using your new email address.

To Sum Up:

- Paid email providers are more professional and more secure.

- Use Hushmail if you want to highest possible security for client files; otherwise use Google Apps.

- If nothing else, make sure you have a professional-sounding free email account.

Design Your Therapy Site

Few therapists would consider running a clinic that had nothing but folding chairs and bare walls.

Yet many therapist sites are poorly designed, difficult to navigate or just plain ugly. That's the digital equivalent of bare walls and folding chairs

Fortunately, your website can escape this fate. Read on to discover how.

Web Design for Therapy Clinics

What would you say if I asked about your goals for your therapy website?

You might say you want your website to look clean and professional, yet reflect your unique personality. You might say you want your website to teach clients about you and your background, or offer information on the different conditions that you treat.

All these answers are fine, but they miss the point. This is what your website should do:

Your website should get clients to book their first session with you.

Everything else is secondary to that goal.

See, here's the thing. When a prospective client comes to your website, they don't want to look at a fancy website. They don't want to learn about your therapeutic orientation. **They want to get help with their problem.**

So your website's job is to direct them to book a therapy session with you, because therapy is where they'll find the help they are looking for. Everything on your website needs to support that goal.

When designing each element of your website, ask yourself

1. "Would this help encourage a client to book their first session?"
2. "Would this distract a client from booking their first session?"

If a particular element does not encourage clients to book their first session (or worse, distracts them from that goal), then you should fix it!

Of course, your website shouldn't consist solely of a big button that says, "Book a session now!" Clients usually want to learn something about you before they book their first session. So it's a good idea to have information about your professional background and the services you offer. You can even include a blog or some videos to show clients your personality and therapeutic style.

But remember to keep the main thing the main thing. Everything on the site — your biography, your blog, etc — should lead a client towards the decision to book their first session.

That's the big idea of designing an effective therapy website. Now let's put it in practice

Best Practices for Therapy Websites

After looking at dozens of therapist websites and seeing common mistakes repeated over and over, I've developed this list of best practices. Each of these guidelines increase the chance that a client will book a session with you after visiting your website.

Throughout this section, I'll be linking to actual websites as visual examples. If you would prefer to click on the URLs instead of typing them out, you can read this section on my website at Marketing-ForTherapists.org/web-design-therapy-clinics.

When I link to websites, I am using them as one specific example. I don't intend to make a statement about the website as a whole, or the therapist behind the website. So don't read too much into my links – they're examples, nothing more. Also, remember that websites do change, and so it's possible that my links will become outdated in time.

I'll explain each best practice in detail, but here is a summary to get you oriented.

- Grab their attention above the fold
- Make your text big
- Get a professional photo

- Make your website mobile-friendly
- Avoid social media buttons
- Don't use carousels
- Avoid psychobabble
- Break text into easily readable chunks
- Make it easy for people to book a session & find your fees
- Get specific feedback

Ready? Let's dive in.

Grab Their Attention Above The Fold

"The fold" is the part of your website that is visible without the user scrolling down. According to Moz.com, users spend 80% of their time looking at the content above the fold. So you need to grab their attention with the content that's visible right away.

In order to grab their attention, you need to present them with a clear reason why they should stick around on your website. The content you put above the fold should be:

- Visually appealing
- Descriptive of what you offer or who you are
- A clear indicator of what the client should do next.
- Uncluttered and free from distracting content

A perfect example is Front Range Counseling (frontrangecounseling-center.com). As soon as you load the page, you see a few paragraphs that summarize what they offer, a photo of a happy family, and a big "contact us" button. I guarantee that many people who visit this website end up becoming clients.

Here's another example of someone who is doing this well — Dr. Keely Kolmes (drkkolmes.com). The top of her page includes a photo of her, a short summary of what she does, her contact information, and a button you can use to subscribe to her mailing list. Within the first six seconds of landing on her page, you already have a decent sense of who she is and what you should do next.

Austin Therapy For Girls (AustinTherapyForGirls.com) is another good example. They have an attractive photo, a quick summary of what they offer, and a "learn more" link that takes you to a page where you can book an appointment.

Unfortunately, there are some bad examples as well.

For instance, Elizabeth O'Brien (elizabethobrienlpc.com) dedicates almost the entire area above the fold to a photo of a flower. It's a nice flower, to be sure, but there are better uses of that space. She could make better use of the space above the fold if she brought her biography up and made it the first thing that visitors saw.

Make Your Text Big

Nobody wants to squint to read your website. Make your font size 16px or so. If you're not sure what that means, just make it bigger than the default. This goes for your menu too — make it big!

Downtown Seattle Counseling (Downtown-seattle-counseling.com) has a tiny font size. My Chicago Counselor (Mychicagocounselor.com) has a nice big font size. Which website would you rather read?

And it's not just about readability. It's also about the image you present as a counselor. Legible font makes your website feel friendly and welcoming. Tiny fonts that people have to squint to read makes your website feel unfriendly. Help people feel welcomed, and pick a good font size.

Get a Professional Photo

Seriously. Hire a professional photographer to get a headshot. Don't use your iPhone, don't take a selfie, and don't grab an old vacation photo from Facebook. Hire a pro.

Then put your photo on your site! Ideally, you should stick it above the fold so people can form a connection with you right away. But it's fine to put the photo on your "About Me" page as well. Just make sure it's professional quality.

Also, think twice before you use stock photography. People are likely to connect with a genuine photo of you or your office. A stock photo of a random person? Not so much.

Make your Website Mobile-Friendly

People use the internet on their mobile devices more than on their computers. So it's essential that your website is mobile-friendly.

Fortunately, this is pretty simple to do. The web-speak term for a mobile-friendly website is "responsive." So you need to make sure that whatever theme, template, or software you use to build your website, it's "responsive".

For instance, if you're using WordPress, you need to pick a theme. When you find a good theme, look at the description and make sure they say it's "responsive." The two Wordpress themes I recommend later in this book are both responsive.

Not sure if your website's current design is responsive? Just use Google's mobile friendly tool (Google.com/webmasters/tools/mobile-friendly) to check. If your website is mobile-friendly, the tool will tell you. You can also pull your website up on your own mobile phone and see how it looks.

Avoid Social Media Sharing Buttons

Just don't do it. Are your clients really going to go on Facebook and say "Hey guys, check out this great therapist I found?" It's fine to discreetly link to your own social media profiles, but you should never have buttons encouraging visitors to share the page.

Don't Use Carousels

A "carousel" in website-talk is when you have a space on your website that multiple pieces of content (usually images) rotate through. It's a very bad idea (visit Shouldiuseacarousel.com if you don't believe me.)

Check out Newman Clinical Associates (Newmanclinical.com). Their entire space above the fold is taken up with their carousel. The problem? Before you can finish reading one carousel image, it goes away (in a blinding white flash), and the next carousel image loads. It's an ineffective way to present the information.

Plus, the information that comes later in the carousel is often missed. Their carousel has a slide about intern supervision, but it doesn't show up right away. I'm guessing most interns that come looking for supervision quickly scan the menu, decide there is no supervision available, and leave before the carousel ever gets to the slide about supervision.

Bottom line: Don't use carousels. If you must use carousels, at least set them so that users can advance through them at will instead of having them automatically scroll. But really, you are better off never using them.

Illustrate with Images

A few images go a long way towards grabbing your readers' attention. They make your writing look more professional and (more importantly) they help you fight against the constant temptation to click away.

So add photos to your writing. You might include one photo at the top of the article, or sprinkle smaller photos throughout the page.

How do you find images? Well, you need to be careful, because most photos you find on the internet are copyright protected. While it's unlikely you'll be caught, you want to be ethical. So it's important to use images that are legally free for anyone to use.

The easiest option is to use a site like Pixabay.com or Unsplash.com. Both sites allow you to search a huge collection of totally free images. If you need more, search Google for "attribution free images" or do some research on finding Creative Commons images.

Once you've found a good source of free images, how do you choose which one to include? Well, there's three things to keep in mind:

- Look for images that relate to what you're writing about. The connection doesn't need to be exact – if you're writing an article about mindfulness exercises, you don't actually need a photo of a therapist teaching someone mindfulness. You could just have a photo of a calm nature scene or a relaxed person.

- Pick images that are appealing to look at. This means you should choose photos that are high-resolution, not blurry, etc. But this also means you should avoid shocking or upsetting images. If you want to write a post about self-harm, don't include a photo of someone's self-harm injury!

- Try to create a theme. While you don't need to have identical images on each page, it's ideal if your images are on related topics, or have a similar visual feel. For instance, you might fill your site with primarily nature images, or mostly images in the same art style.

Avoid Psychobabble

Your clients probably don't know what a therapeutic orientation is, and they probably don't care.

But they do care about whether you will give them lots of advice or mainly just listen. They do care about whether you plan to explore their past or focus more on changing their current behavior.

So tell them those things. Instead of giving them a lesson on your theoretical orientation, tell them what therapy with you will be like. Don't get philosophical or pie-in-the-sky; focus on real questions your clients bring.

Theoretical orientation is just one example of areas where psychobabble can creep in. Be on the guard for other topics where you might be tempted to use psychobabble, such as your discussion of the conditions you treat.

Of course, it's fine to use psychobabble if your intended audience is other professionals. For instance, if you speak at professional conferences, other therapists might visit your website to learn more about your expertise.

If that's the case, have a separate page on your site called "For Professionals" and keep the main area of your website focused on the clients. Kristin Lanning's page (Kristinlanningcounseling.com/for-professionals.html) is a good example of this.

Break Text into Easily Readable Chunks

You might have noticed that most paragraphs in this book are only a few sentences long.

This is because short chunks of text are much easier to read on the web. For instance, compare Dr. Nakisher's bio (Chicagotherapist.com/steven-nakisher-team-1.php) with Dr Aber's bio (Counselingandtherapy-psychologist.com/Therapist-Chicago-Counselor.html). Dr. Nakisher's bio is much easier to read, because the content is chunked into short paragraphs. The large headings don't hurt either.

Make it Easy for People to Book a Session & Find Your Fees

If it's unclear how to book a session, many clients will leave your website without contacting you.

So make it really, *really* easy for clients to book a session with you. Louis Laves-Webb (louislaves-webb.com) does a great job with this. His office has a bar at the top of their site with information on booking a session, and his home page has a big button that says "Book a session now!" Clients who visit his site have two immediately obvious options for booking a session. Your website should have at least one.

Similarly, you need to make it obvious what your fees are. Have a page in your menu that says something like "Fees" or "Insurance & Fees" or something like that. Don't make people dig to find out whether or not they can afford you. If you prefer to not publish your fees, you should at least have a page on whether or not you accept insurance.

Get Specific Feedback

Ask friends, family and colleagues for feedback on your site.

Don't just show it to them and ask "What do you think?" because you don't want flattery. Instead, ask them specific questions.

Ask them things like, "If you were a client, what would make you choose me as a therapist, or pass on me as a therapist?" Ask them to imagine they are a particular kind of client (for instance, a client with depression, a low-income client, an elderly client) and see how well that client would be served by your website. Offer to buy them lunch for every problem they find that you can fix.

You might also try the free service Peek (Peek.Usertesting.com). Peek records a five-minute video of a random stranger using your website and offering their comments. Since the people visiting your website are random users, not website design experts, take their advice with a grain of salt.

Putting It All Together

Whew! This is a lot of information, I know. To review, here are the practices you want to remember:

- Grab their attention above the fold
- Make your text big

- Get a professional photo
- Make your website mobile-friendly
- Avoid social media buttons
- Don't use carousels
- Illustrate with images
- Avoid psychobabble
- Break text into easily readable chunks
- Make it easy for people to book a session & find your fees
- Get specific feedback

Remember, the goal of your website is to encourage clients to book their first session with you. When in doubt, just ask yourself, "What can I do that would make clients more likely to book a session with me?" If you're not sure, ask a friend to use your website and give you their honest feedback.

Also, remember that you don't have to go it alone. I'm available to help with your web design, so if you're feeling overwhelmed, just drop me a line at MarketingForTherapists.org/Contact and we'll improve your website together.

Attract New Clients

If you've followed all the steps in the guide, by now you've launched your therapy website.

That's a fantastic accomplishment! You are well on your way to online marketing success.

But you're not there yet. The next step is to make sure clients discover your fantastic new site. That's what we'll tackle next – starting with search engine optimization, and moving on to therapist directories and social media. Because I have so much to say about online advertising, I'll cover it at the end of the book.

SEO Guide for Therapists

Most people begin their search for a therapist on Google.

So if you want people to find you, you need to show up in the Google search results. Unfortunately, you can't call up Google ask them nicely to put you at the top of the search results. Instead, you need to convince Google's algorithm that your website is the most relevant website for a particular search. That's where SEO comes in.

SEO stands for search engine optimization. Google's algorithm looks at a huge amount of data to determine the best pages to show to each searcher. SEO refers to all the things you can do to give Google's algorithm the impression that your site deserves to be included in the results when someone searches for a therapist.

A Metaphor For SEO

Let's say you are a tour guide, and your business depends on referrals from local travel agents. You want the travel agents to send you as many clients as possible.

So what could you do to convince the travel agents to send people to your tour?

First, you build a positive **reputation** for your tour. If lots of people agree your tour is fun, word will get to the travel agents, and they'll be more likely to recommend you.

Second, you want to give the travel agents **information about your tours**. For instance, you might send them a brochure that lists all the tours you offer, along with prices and locations.

Finally, you want the tour itself to be **as good as possible** because undercover employees of the travel agents will occasionally visit your tour and report back on the quality.

Making sense so far? Great, then SEO will make sense too.

On a basic level, SEO consists of three factors: Getting a positive **reputation** online, giving the search engines lots of **information about your site**, and making your site **as good as possible**. We'll explore each of those factors in turn.

Beyond the basic level, things are much more complex. I'm leaving out many advanced concepts to keep things as accessible as possible. If you'd like a more in-depth guide to SEO, check out the guides I list in my recommended resources.

Getting a Good Reputation Online

Google determines your online reputation by looking at the links other sites send to your site. Google treats each link as an endorsement — if someone is linking to you, it implies your site is valuable in some way. This means that a big part of your SEO strategy should be encouraging others to link to you. The more people that link to you, the more evidence Google has that your site is credible.

However, not all links are created equal. You would trust information on harvard.edu much more than you would trust information on a random blog — and for good reason! Similarly, Google values links differently depending on the credibility of the website they come from.

If Harvard links to you, your credibility in Google's eyes will increase quite a bit. But if your Aunt Irma's cat blog links to you, Google probably won't care much.

In fact, Google has systems in place to detect attempts to fool its algorithm, so if you ask Aunt Irma to start 50 cat blogs and link them all to you, Google might even penalize your website as punishment. So you want as many votes as possible, from sites that are trustworthy and authoritative.

Also, Google looks at more than just the authority of the website linking to you. It also looks at the relevancy between that website and your website. For instance, even if Aunt Irma had the most popular cat blog in the world, a link from her to your therapy clinic would still not be worth much. She has a lot of cat related authority, but not much therapy-related authority.

However, if you launched a new pet food line, then a link from Aunt Irma's cat blog would be very valuable, because her website would have high authority and be relevant to the topic of your website.

Here's what it means when you put this all together:

Build your clinic's reputation by attracting links from trustworthy, relevant sites.

By trustworthy, I mean websites that are reputable and have many other websites linking to them. By relevant, I mean websites that relate to your clinic in some way — such as websites that discuss mental health or websites that talk about your local area.

How do you attract links? Here are five easy ways

1. Ask nicely. This works best when you have a connection to the person or organization you're asking. For instance, if you have a colleague with a different specialty than you, the two of you might agree to link to each other's websites. If you are on the board of directors for a mental health nonprofit, see if they can link to your website from your bio on their website.

2. Guest blog. Does someone run a mental health blog? See if you can write an article for them, and get a link back to your site in return

3. Mention someone else on your website. For instance, let's say you read someone's book on mindfulness and write a positive book review on your clinic's blog. Email the author of the book and let them know — perhaps they would link to your review!

4. Submit your website to all relevant directories for your area. Google My Business (Google.com/Business), Yelp, and your local chamber of commerce are all great ideas.

5. Make genuinely useful content that people will want to link to. If you write a particularly helpful article, people might share the link without you even needing to ask.

And here are three ways you should *never* try to get links:

1. Never pay for links. There are some skeezy companies out there that will offer to place links on various websites if you

pay them. That might have worked years ago, but Google is wise to those tricks now, and you'll just be wasting your money.

2. Never spam your website on blog comments or forum posts. It's okay to mention your website if it's relevant, but generally Google ignores links in comments or forum posts — and in any case, this kind of unsolicited self-promotion looks really unprofessional.

3. Never pay to submit your website to any directories. Again, years ago directories were valuable, but nowadays Google generally ignores them. The exception is local directories that people actually use. For instance, if your local chamber of commerce has a directory, by all means, submit your website to it. But these local directories are normally totally free. If you have to pay, steer clear.

Giving Search Engines Information About Your Site

Adding Keywords To Your Pages

Let's imagine that Dr. Smith launches a brand new website for his site. On his front page, it says:

"Welcome! I'm glad you stopped by. My name is Dr. Smith, and I'm here to help. My goal is to provide a safe and compassionate place where clients can get encouragement and support as they navigate through the challenges of life. No matter what you're going through, there is hope. Please contact me to set up a session today!"

What's the problem here? Simple. There's nothing in this paragraph that tells Google that Dr. Smith is a therapist. What's more, there's nothing that tells Google what kinds of conditions Dr. Smith treats, or where he's located.

That means that if someone searches for "local anxiety therapist", Dr. Smith is not likely to show up.

We can solve this problem by sprinkling certain phrases (which are called "keywords" in SEO-talk) into our website. Google can use these keywords to figure out what our site is about. For instance, we might rewrite Dr. Smith's website to say something like this: (changes in bold)

*"Welcome! I'm glad you stopped by. My name is Dr. Smith, and I'm here to help. My goal as a **therapist** is to provide a safe and compassionate place where **counseling** clients from **all over Chicago** can get encouragement and support as they navigate through the challenges of life. No matter what you're going through, **whether depression, anxiety, or PTSD**, there is hope. Please contact me to set up a session today!"*

See what I did? The overall meaning of the page was preserved, but we added keywords that tell Google who Dr. Smith is and what he offers.

Of course, you don't want to go overboard. If Dr. Smith rewrote his website to say:

"Welcome! I'm glad you stopped by to my Chicago anxiety clinic. My name is Dr Smith, and I'm a Chicago anxiety therapist. My goal as a Chicago anxiety therapist is to provide a safe and compassionate place where anxiety clients in Chicago can get encouragement and support from their local Chicago anxiety therapist as they navigate through the challenges of life as a Chicago anxiety client...."

It would almost certainly backfire. For one thing, Google can detect when someone is doing this (they call it "keyword stuffing.") For another thing, a client who comes to this website will be immediately scared off by.

The bottom line:

- You should sprinkle some keywords into your pages, but in moderation. If your writing starts to suffer, it's a sure sign you're adding too many keywords.

- Your keyword should reflect the conditions you treat, and the area you live in.

- Use a variety of keywords for the same topic. For instance, if you treat eating disorders, you should not only use the phrase "eating disorders" but also use "anorexia" and "bulimia." That way your page is relevant no matter how someone writes their search.

Creating New Pages For Keywords

Ever heard of "jack of all trades, master of none?" That principle applies to SEO as well. If you have a massive homepage that talks about all the different conditions you treat, it's likely Google will look at that page as being sort-of relevant for all of those conditions, but not incredibly relevant for any of them.

However, if you have an individual page for each condition you specialize in, then Google is more likely to decide that your individual pages deserve to be shown when someone searches for those specific conditions.

Don't go overboard on this, though. For this technique to be effective, your pages need to be detailed and well-made, and you should ideally try to get links to your individual pages. That's a lot of work!

It's better to focus on two or three pages for the conditions that you most want to focus on, rather than dilute your effort across every single condition you potentially treat. You can always add more pages later on.

Also, make sure that these pages talk about your geographic location. Your clients will usually search for a therapist in their area, so it's important that your individual pages are not about "depression treatment" but "[my city] depression treatment."

Add Keywords To Your URL

This is an easy trick to give Google more information about your pages (and make your site look classier to boot).

All you need to do is make sure the URL for a particular page reflects the content of that page. For instance, if you have a contact page, make the URL example.com/contact. Simple, right?

You can take this to the level by making the URLs extra descriptive. For instance, let's say you have a page about depression treatment, and you've decided to give it the url example.com/depression. That's okay, but it would be better to make the url example.com/depression-treatment or example.com/Atlanta-depression-treatment. That way you're signaling to Google that your page isn't just about depression, it's about the treatment of depression (in Atlanta!). Again, no need to go overboard here. Adding two to four description words in your URL is plenty.

Add Your Address

This one is pretty straightforward. Put your address and phone number on every page, either in your header or your footer. That gives Google a very clear signal that you are located at a particular address, which means it will be more likely to show your website to clients near you.

If your website design doesn't allow you to add your address and phone number to every page, at least put your full address on your contact page. But every page is preferred.

Get Listed on Google My Business

Google My Business is Google's own directory for local businesses. Google uses the information in that directory whenever anyone does a search for a local business (like a local therapist!)

A Google My Business listing allows you to add a description of your business and photos of your business. Having an updated Google My Business listing will make it more likely that your business shows up in Google Maps results and in Google search results.

When you create your Google My Business page, try to include some high-quality photos of the clinic, and use a detailed description that includes specific keywords related to your business. For instance, "Acme counseling center provides compassionate therapy to individuals suffering from mental health issues such as depression, anxiety, and PTSD. Our therapists and counselors are all trained at the master's or doctoral level, and we have been in the local area for over ten years."

You can sign up at Google.com/business.

Make Your Site as Helpful as Possible

Ok, what does it mean to make your site as helpful as possible?

Simple. Your website needs to have quality, helpful content that goes beyond just trying to book sessions.

Think of it like this. There's two bike shops in your city. One bike shop is staffed by employees who will sell you a bike and do nothing else. The other bike shop is staffed by employees who are happy to answer your questions about biking, teach you the best bike routes around town, and generally share lots of information with you — even if you don't make a purchase.

Which bike shop would you rather go to? The second one, obviously. The first bike shop just exists to sell bikes, whereas the second one is genuinely helpful.

Your website should be like the second bike shop. It's great for your website to list the services that you offer and give information on your professional background. But you should go beyond that. Write content that would be genuinely helpful to people, even if they never book a session with you.

For instance, you might write an article about what to look for in a therapist, or an article about how mindfulness can help with social anxiety. You might write some reviews of your favorite books on depression, or record videos where you take people through a virtual relaxation exercise. These are just a few examples — I'm sure you can think of more.

The key with this content is to make it truly valuable. Take the time to make your writing as strong as it can be. Provide well-developed pages that are at least 600 words long.

Also, try to make your content unique. Many other websites already describe the symptoms of depression, so you're not adding anything new if you also write about that exact topic. But what if you write about depression amongst an underserved population? That will increase the chances that your content is unique and truly helpful.

Having this valuable content boosts your SEO efforts in two ways. First, people might reference your content on their websites, which gives you more links. Second, quality content makes your website stand out to Google, and increases their confidence that you are a relevant result for their searchers.

If you want to put this in practice, I recommend choosing a topic that you can write 5-10 articles about. Many therapists write lots of blog posts on random topics, but it's better to explore one topic in depth.

For instance, write five articles on managing anxiety, with each article covering something different (using mindfulness to combat anxiety, seeking therapy for anxiety, different kinds of anxiety, medication for anxiety, etc). You'll create a helpful resource for clients, and you'll appear more authoritative to Google.

Of course, not everyone enjoys writing. If you want to add content to your website but don't want to write it yourself, consider hiring a ghostwriter. I recommend my friend Kyler who runs WritingForTherapists.org. He's a graduate student in clinical psychology (like me!), so he's knowledgeable about therapy. And he's affordable compared to professional ghostwriters.

Oh, one more thing. The best content in the world doesn't do you any good if your website takes forever to load. A good goal is to make sure your website loads in three seconds or less. Test your page load speed at GtMetrix.com. Google's algorithm uses page load time to determine if your site is quality or not and (more importantly) your visitors will leave your site if it loads too slowly.

If your page speed is too slow, there are several things you can do. The easiest is to use smaller images. If you are using Wordpress, consider using a caching plugin like WP Super Cache, or switching to a better host such as WPEngine.

Summary

Okay, I know this is a lot of information — but it will start making sense as you put it into practice.

Just remember the tour guide metaphor. You want a good reputation. You want to give travel agents plenty of information about your tours. And you want your tours to be as good as possible.

Apply that to SEO. You build your reputation by having other quality sites link to you. You give agents information by including relevant keywords in your pages, including your address on your website, and signing up for directories like Google My Business. Finally, you make your tours as good as possible by writing lengthy, high-quality articles on valuable topics.

As you do these things, your site will become higher-quality in Google's eyes, and you'll start to get more and more traffic from search engines. Good luck!

Social Media for Therapists

As a therapist, there are three main reasons you shouldn't give much of your attention to social media.

First, social media opens you up to potential ethical problems. Dr. Keely Kolmes has done an excellent run-down of the potential pitfalls of social media for clinicians at Drkkolmes.com/clinician-articles. The last thing you need is to be hauled before an ethics board because you tweeted personally identifiable information about a client.

Second, social media just doesn't work very well for therapy clinics. Other types of businesses can tweet coupons, engage with followers, or ask customers to share the business with their friends. As an ethical therapist, you probably can't do any of those things. Sure, you can post your own thoughts, but you'll miss out on the "social" part of social media.

Third, social media requires a large time investment in order to attract followers. You need to follow lots of other people, you need to participate in lots of discussions, and you need to aggressively encourage people to follow you. All of that takes time you could be spending elsewhere in the business.

If you ask me, you are better off using that time to improve your website, study new therapy techniques, or takes some self-care time.

However, I don't think you should ignore social media entirely. I've got a strategy for social media that will allow you to reap most of the benefits with a small commitment of a few hours to get set up, and then an hour a month or so.

For my strategy, you'll use Linkedin and Twitter, and ignore everything else.

LinkedIn

Like it or hate it, LinkedIn is an essential tool for professional connections. And by professional connections, I mean "people who will help you find a job."

It's also handy for establishing your professional credibility in general, which is useful if you want to be invited to speak at a conference or teach a CE course. So even if you're not planning on job hunting anytime soon, LinkedIn is still worth a visit.

My LinkedIn strategy is pretty straightforward.

1. Set up a killer profile

2. Check it once a year and update if needed

3. Connect with colleagues. (Don't connect with clients!)

#2 and #3 are pretty self-explanatory, but you'll probably need a little help on #1. Here's how you make a great LinkedIn profile.

How to Make a Fantastic LinkedIn Profile

An excellent profile is not difficult to make. Here's what you need to do:

Step One: Get a professional photo

Your photo is the first thing that people will see when they open your LinkedIn profile. Make sure it's a good one.

Ideally, you would hire a professional photographer to take your photo. But if you can't afford that, here are some tips for making sure your photo makes a great impression:

- Dress professionally. Save the jeans and t-shirt for Facebook. Your LinkedIn photo should show you dressed like you would for an interview.

- Avoid blurry or dim photos.

- Don't have anyone else in the photo – and we can tell if you cropped them out.

- Focus on just your head, or your head and upper body. If the photo is of your entire body, it will be hard to recognize you in the thumbnail.

- Make sure you have a professional background. A blank wall or an outdoor scene is fine. A bar or your living room, not so much.

Step Two: Fill out your experience

The Experience section of LinkedIn is essentially your resume. Most people are unlikely to read it in depth – who really cares about the job you had ten years ago? But many people will skim through it to get a sense of who you are and what you can offer, so it pays to make sure this section is filled out.

Remember though, you're writing it for people who will probably skim. So write it to highlight your accomplishments. Think quality over quantity. Try to include every position (so there are no strange gaps in your timeline), but include only the important details. If it's not interesting, delete it.

A good way of writing your experience section is to have a one or two sentence summary of each position, plus 3-5 bullet points detailing your biggest accomplishments or most impressive responsibilities in that position.

Another way is to have three short paragraphs (1-2 sentences each.) One paragraph which summarizes the position, one which lists your significant accomplishments, and one which talks about the skills you developed or displayed. For instance, if I listed writing this post as a position on LinkedIn, I might say:

LinkedIn Profile Guru

As a LinkedIn Profile Guru, I helped readers build a perfect LinkedIn profile.

My LinkedIn profile advice was read by over 100,000 people, and helped lead to the creation of 500 new LinkedIn profiles.

As a LinkedIn profile guru, my success was driven by my ability to develop expert LinkedIn strategies, write in a style that was clear and enjoyable to read, and incorporate feedback from my editors.

You can pick whatever format works best for you, as long as you make sure your experience section is easy to skim.

Here's a quick test. Show your experience section to a friend for thirty seconds and then ask them what they remember from it. If their answer doesn't include any of your impressive accomplishments or traits, rewrite. Remember that you don't need an impressive job to have impressive accomplishments – a hiring director is likely to be interested in someone who did a great job in a boring position, or a student who was achieved something significant in a routine class.

Step Three: Write a fantastic summary

This is where you'll be spending most of your time with LinkedIn.

Your summary is the first thing people read, and it's the only thing most of them will read.

So make it good.

Put it in first person. Everyone knows you wrote it yourself so it's weird if your summary says "Dr. Cruz is a psychotherapist specializing in blah blah blah."

Tell a story. Don't give bullet points, and don't just summarize your resume. Instead, give a sense of who you are. Talk about your specialties, your passions, your strengths.

Also, have an intended audience in mind. What kind of person do you most want to impress with your LinkedIn summary? Is it possible employers? Conference organizers? Colleagues? Keep that intended audience in mind as you write.

An easy way to make this work is a three paragraph format.

Your first paragraph should be just one sentence long. It should summarize the absolutely most essential information about you.

Your second paragraph tells the story of your work history. Key word here is STORY. Don't tell every detail — just give the most important information.

Finally, your last paragraph should summarize your skills and strengths. This is your chance to talk about the things you're really good at, and the areas where you're passionate.

Optionally, you can conclude with a single sentence call to action.

Here's what this looks like:

LinkedIn Summary Example

I'm Doctor Smith, and I have been helping clients overcome anxiety for over a decade.

I currently lead the Acme anxiety clinic, where I manage a team of seven licensed clinicians, as well as one pre-doctoral intern. I also consult with the local city council on a public mental health outreach program that has reduced involuntary psychiatric holds by 30%.

I'm deeply passionate about the work that I do, and I thrive on the opportunity to help clients achieve freedom from their anxiety. I also love investing in the development of other clinicians, and cherish the opportunity to lead my colleagues at the Acme clinic.

I'm available to speak on best practices for anxiety treatment, and I encourage you to email me at smith@example.com if interested.

Easy, right? Now, let's tackle Twitter.

Twitter

LinkedIn mattered because of your opportunity to connect with colleagues. Twitter matters because of your opportunity to connect with clients.

Of course, you won't communicate directly with clients on Twitter — remember your ethics! But your clients are naturally curious about their therapists, so if you have a Twitter profile, some of your clients will find it and read it (especially if you link to it from your homepage.)

This creates an opportunity for you. Most clients are looking for a therapist they can connect with. If your Twitter account demonstrates some of your personality, you might help a prospective client feel some rapport with you. And if you are able to share insightful thoughts that show your expertise, clients might feel you are a trustworthy expert.

Of course, you don't want to go overboard here. You want to remain professional even while you show personality. If in doubt, have a friend or colleague look through your posts before you send them. But if your Twitter account gives clients a sense of who you are, it might make them more likely to book an initial session with you.

Also, a word on ethics: Even though your clients might be reading your Twitter, you should not use Twitter to communicate with clients, and you shouldn't follow your clients (even if they follow you first.) And of course, don't discuss clients on Twitter, even if you remove identifying information. If you share a story about a client on Twitter, you run the risk that client will read it. Err on the side of safety.

Connect with Colleagues On Twitter

Of course, you can use Twitter for professional connections, too. It's a bit less formal than LinkedIn, so it's a nice way to establish friendly connections with colleagues.

Twitter is an especially good way to keep connected with other clinicians you meet at workshops or conferences. Swapping business cards is nice, but it's easy to lose contact. However, if you follow someone on Twitter (or they follow you), you'll keep popping up in each other's feed on occasion. This keeps the connection warm, and makes it easier to reestablish contact later.

Plus, if you speak at a conference or workshop, you can put your Twitter in your professional bio. That's an easy way to build followers and establish some credibility. Even if you're not a speaker, you could include your Twitter name on your business cards.

If you read other guides on Twitter, they'll sometimes talk about becoming a "thought leader" on Twitter. This is mostly hogwash. Nobody is going to suddenly offer you a book deal because you've got 50 followers, or even 5,000. Use Twitter as a tool to connect with your existing colleagues, and don't worry too much about being a "thought leader."

Twitter in One Hour a Month

Ok, so how do you use Twitter without it wasting your time?

The answer is a nifty website called Buffer (Buffer.com). Buffer allows you to write a bunch of Twitter posts at once, and then send them out over time. So you can write 12 posts, tell Buffer to send out one a week, and you're set for three months. Your Twitter account stays active, but you don't need to touch it. Best of all, Buffer is free and super easy to use.

What should you write your posts about? Well, I recommend a mix:

- Send out some links to helpful resources. For instance, you might tweet a link to a helpful book or article about coping with depression.
- Share an inspirational or encouraging quote
- Write your own inspirational or encouraging thoughts
- Share a link to a song you like
- Share a funny video
- Share some of your thoughts about being a therapist

Again, keep it professional — but show your personality, and try to be helpful. You'll get the hang of it pretty soon. If you're not sure what to write about, ask some friends, or look at what other therapists are doing.

In summary, here's the official MarketingForTherapists.org Twitter plan:

1. Stay professional, but let your personality shine through

2. Use Buffer to schedule several weeks (or months) of posts in advance. Once it runs dry, write another batch.

3. Get off Twitter and do something meaningful with your life!

Everything else

Ok, what about everything else? What about Facebook or Pinterest or whatever newfangled social network is popular today?

My advice is simple: Ignore them.

You can easily sink hours into building and updating social media profiles, but it's doubtful if that time will bring you a single client. If you're like most clinicians, you have no shortage of responsibilities demanding your time, and it's foolish to squander hours chasing Facebook likes. So save the stress, and ignore everything but Twitter and LinkedIn.

Of course, if there is a good reason for you to ignore this advice, then go ahead! If your colleague has had great success with a Facebook page for her clinic, give it a try. If you read a great blog post about Pinterest marketing, feel free to explore.

But treat it as an experiment. Keep track the hours you are putting into this new social media platform, and be careful to record everything. (Ten minutes here and there adds up over time.)

After your new platform has been running for a few weeks, look at your results and compare it to the hours you've invested. If you've put in five hours and gotten five likes, ask yourself if your time is worth more than one like per hour.

Also, remember that the only thing that ultimately matters is new clients. Even if you received thousands of new likes on social media, they don't help your business unless they lead to new clients.

Therapist Directories

Therapist directories allow clients to search a list of all therapists in their area. They're one of the most common marketing tools that therapists use, so you may have already signed up for a directory. Because they're so popular, it's difficult for your directory entry to stand out. I wrote this guide to help.

What Directory To Use?

The 800 pound gorilla is Psychology Today, and the up-and-coming underdog is Goodtherapy. There are other directories out there, but I wouldn't bother with them since Psychology Today and Goodtherapy have pretty much cornered the market. They both cost about $300 a year, which means they're probably worthwhile if they send you a handful of clients each year. Between the two, there's no clearly superior option. I would try both for one year and see which sends you more clients.

Also, before you sign up, see if you can get a free trial. Right now you can get a free 6-month trial to Psychology Today's directory using PEPPERDINE as your coupon code. If that code is expired, do a Google search for "psychology today directory free trial" and see if you find any deals.

How to Stand Out

There are tons of therapists on both directories, so you need to stand out if you want to get clients. Here's a few things you should keep in mind.

Research Your Competition

Before your build out your profile, go on the directory and search for your own zip code. See what everyone else is doing. Imagine you are a client, and figure out which profiles would attract you and which you would ignore. Don't go in blind — look at the other therapists who will be competing for your clients' attention.

Get A Good Photo

Seriously. If your photo is low-res, blurry, or you've got a weird expression on your face, clients won't click on you. I've said it before and I'll say it again — invest in a quality headshot from a professional photographer.

Optimize your first 2-3 lines

Both Goodtherapy and Psychology Today pull the first few lines from your profile to use in the search results. Goodtherapy uses your first line and a half (about 150 characters) while Psychology Today uses your first three lines (about 200 characters) That means that you should write those first few lines to grab the attention of someone who is scrolling through the directory.

In other words, if you start your profile by defining therapy, listing your educational background, or blasting people with a bunch of psychobabble, that's the content that will end up in your search result — and probably, nobody will click on it.

Instead, try writing your first 2-3 lines to grab people's attention. Some ideas:

- Give concrete examples of your expertise. Anyone can say "I specialize in depression" but not everyone can say "I have treated depression for over 25 years" or "I have given over a dozen lectures on depression."

- If you have a unique specialty, put that front and center. It's okay to mention that you do other things too, but most of your description should be about your specialty.

- Consider using questions. Last time I checked, almost no-body was using questions at the beginning of their profile. It can be difficult to craft a succinct question that relates to your services, but give it a try. Questions help you stand out, and they grab the attention of prospective clients.

Try for A Conversational Tone

If you look at most of the profiles on Psychology Today or Good Therapy, they're overtly formal and full of technical jargon. If you're able to write with an authentic, friendly, and conversational tone, clients will be drawn to your profile.

So here's what I recommend. Sit down with a good friend, and maybe a glass of wine (or whatever helps you relax.) Then have your friend ask you questions about your practice. Why do you like being a therapist? What is your hope for your clients? What's the number one thing you'd want a prospective client to know about you? Etc. Answer their questions in an unfiltered way, and have a camera record the conversation.

Then go back and review the video. When you find a great answer, write it down word-for-word. Then put it into your profile, and edit it to clean up the rough edges. This will help you communicate your true personality in your profile.

Oh, and one more thing — after you've done this, have the same friend look at the profile. Make sure they agree that the profile reflects your real self, and is sufficiently professional. This prevents you from creating a profile that is too conversational and not professional enough.

Track Your Results

How do you know if a directory is worth the money? See how many clients it brings you.

Both directories give you some information about people who have visited your site or contacted you through the directory. But you should go one step beyond that and actually track how many customers found you through the directory. The high-tech way is to look at your website's analytics data, and see how many visitors from a directory fill out your contact form. The low-tech way is to have an optional box on your intake form asking people how they found out about you.

Either option will give you valuable insight into how many clients are actually coming your way from these directories. If you find that a directory isn't bringing you enough clients to justify the price you're paying, take another look at your profile to see if there are any ways you can improve or optimize it.

If you've already done everything you can do to the profile and you're still not getting enough business, it's probably time to cancel your membership and focus your marketing attempts elsewhere. You can always try again in a year or two, after some of your competition might have moved away or stopped paying for their directory profile. Remember, therapy directories should only be a small piece of your overall marketing efforts, so it's okay if they don't work for you.

Protect Your Privacy

In the previous section, I taught you how to attract attention online. In this section, I'll teach you how to prevent attention from landing on your personal information.

Strictly speaking, protecting your privacy isn't a part of online marketing. Keeping your personal information secure won't bring you new clients. But it will help you sleep better at night, and it only takes a few minutes to protect yourself. So let's take a brief detour and talk about online privacy.

Online Privacy & You

It's wise to control the information that clients can find about you online.

Partially, this is because you want to present a consistent professional image. Do you really want a prospective client to see that video of you singing karaoke after you had a few drinks?

This is also to protect the therapeutic relationship. If a client tells you they discovered something personal about you online, it might make you feel uncomfortable and damage rapport. Even if your therapeutic style is very open, you probably would prefer to choose what you shared with the client, instead of having the client discover things about you on their own.

And finally, it's important for reasons of safety. While I hope you never have a client who has tendencies towards stalking or violence, it could happen. If you have a client who has threatened you, do you really want them to have access to information about your personal life?

Of course, it's okay to have some personal information about you available online. But you want to be aware of what's out there, and you want to carefully consider if you're comfortable with everything that a client could find out about you. If you're not comfortable with something you discover, you want to do your best to remove information that should stay private.

In this day and age, it's probably impossible to remove every scrap of your personal information from the web. But there's three things you can do that will go a long way towards making sure your personal information stays private.

1) Google Your Name

Do a Google search for your name and read the results. Don't just look at the first page – go back three or four pages. You might try the other search engines (Bing, Yahoo) as well.

If nothing from your personal life comes up, then great! You can skip the rest of this section.

But if you find pages that relate to your personal life, your clients might find those pages too. So you'll need to make a decision. Are you comfortable with clients finding out that information about you?

You might find that you are comfortable with the idea. Perhaps you don't mind if clients read an opinion piece you wrote for your local newspaper, or listen to some music you recorded with your college band. If you Google for a friend of mine, one of the first results is a video of him deadlifting 400 pounds. He's proud of this video and doesn't mind clients seeing it at all!

You might also find that you'd rather not have personal information about you online. When my first website (ImproveYourSocial-Skills.com) started to become popular and people started searching for me, I removed my name from an old blog that I had written in high school. There was nothing inappropriate on that blog, but I didn't feel comfortable with strangers potentially reading the things I wrote. Similarly, you might discover personal information that you prefer to keep hidden.

If you decide that you don't want clients to discover the personal information that Google uncovered, you have a few options.

If the personal information is on an account or website that you control (like your personal Instagram account), log in and change the privacy settings. You can remove your name, make it private, or just delete it altogether.

If the personal information resides on a site that someone else controls, see if you can ask them to remove it. Be polite, and remember they are doing you a favor. Don't threaten legal action or else you risk bringing even more attention to the information you want removed.

If you can't remove the personal information, you can try to push it further down in the search results. Most people don't read past the first page of results, so if your personal information shows up on page three or four when someone searches for your name, very few people will ever find it.

The easiest way to do this is by following the advice in my SEO guide earlier in the book. If your website rises in the search results, negative information will naturally fall.

If you have something you desperately need to push down, you might consider hiring a reputation management company. They will create lots of websites, blog posts, etc, to fill the search results with positive portrayals of you. Of course, this is a little skeezy – and quite expensive. But in case you ever need that option, I wanted you to know about it.

By the way, Google offers a free service called Google Alerts (Google.com/alerts). Just enter a topic you'd like to stay updated on, and Google will email you anytime new information about that topic is published.

Sign up to receive alerts on your name, and you'll know as soon as someone publishes something new about you. I also recommend getting alerts on the name of your clinic, as well as any other topics you find interesting. Remember that Google will email you anytime a topic is updated, so don't ask for updates on something like "depression" or you will be inundated.

2) Secure Your Facebook Account

After Google, the next place a client is likely to look for you is on Facebook. Usually this is for innocuous reasons. They probably feel a strong connection with you, and don't realize it's inappropriate to "friend" their therapist. But even though the client may have good intentions, the effect is the same – a breach of the boundary between your professional and personal life.

You might think it's okay to let this slide, but it's important to protect your privacy. Most people have hundreds of photos and years of updates on Facebook. You don't want anyone other than friends and family having access to that information.

The good news is that it only takes a few minutes to secure your Facebook account. Just click the padlock icon in the top right of Facebook after logging in, and you should see privacy options.

The first step is to do the Facebook Privacy Checkup, which is a "guided tour" through some of the more common privacy settings. Then you should look at the advanced options and make sure everything is set the way you want it. In general, you should have your posts, photos and profile information visible to friends only, and you should not allow your profile to be indexed in other search engines. This will prevent clients from seeing your information without adding you as a friend.

Of course, clients can still see your posts if you add them as a friend. So I recommend never adding a client as a friend (and consider removing clients you have already added). If a client requests, you should decline and then tell them in their next session that you have a policy of never adding clients on Facebook.

If you're worried about declining client requests, you can change your profile to use your middle name instead of your last name, or using your last initial instead of your last name. That way clients can't search for you. You can also create a page for your therapy practice, and encourage clients to follow that page instead of friending your personal account.

Oh, and make sure to update your security settings as well. You can reduce the odds that someone will break into your account by doing things like setting up alerts and choosing trusted friends who can get you back into your account if you are locked out. It's not likely that someone will try to break you're your account, but better safe than sorry.

3) Add WHOIS Privacy to Your Domain

When you register a domain name, your name, address, and phone number is stored in something called the WHOIS database. Anyone with an internet connection can visit the database and look up the owner of a domain name. (Try it yourself at whois.icann.org).

The WHOIS database is used for many legitimate purposes. For instance, if someone would like to purchase a domain name that has already been registered, they can use the WHOIS database to get in contact with the owner. Or if a website is doing something illegal, law enforcement can use the WHOIS database to track down the criminal.

Unfortunately, it can also be used by folks with bad intentions. If your home address is stored in the WHOIS database, a disgruntled client could find out exactly where you live. And you're not allowed to put false information in your WHOIS entry. ICANN (the nonprofit organization that oversees the internet) will suspend your website if they catch you adding false information.

Fortunately, there is a solution. Just change your WHOIS information to your business address instead of your personal information. You can update this information by logging into your account at your domain registrar. You will need to change this information if you end up moving offices, but otherwise it should work just fine and keep you protected.

If your office can't accept mail or if you work out of a home office, you can still protect yourself. Domain registrars offer something called WHOIS privacy. Essentially, they allow you to use their contact information in the WHOIS database, and then forward you all the correspondence they receive. This satisfies ICANN's requirement while protecting your privacy.

Registrars usually charge money for this service, but it's fairly affordable. If you use Namecheap as I recommend, it will cost only a few dollars per year. In fact, Namecheap gives you one year of domain privacy for free, so you just need to set that to auto-renew and you are all set.

Most clients will not be aware of the WHOIS database, and very few clients will want to look up your home address. But over the course of your career, you might have at least one client that does – and one is too many!

Protecting your privacy is free if you can use a business address, and only a few dollars a year if you use Namecheap's privacy service. Buy yourself some peace of mind and make sure your WHOIS data is secured.

Action Items:

- Search for your name and try to remove any information you don't want visible.

- Lock down your Facebook privacy settings.

- Pay for WHOIS protection for your websites, or change your WHOIS information to your business address.

Self-Publishing Success

Self-publishing a book can be a fantastic boon to your business. It can bring you new clients, provide a fresh source of income, and build your credibility as an expert.

It's true that writing a book isn't for everyone. You have to put in a lot of time, and there's no guarantee it will ever sell. If you detest the idea of writing, this might not be for you.

But I'd encourage you to consider it. If you had asked me a few years ago, I never would have thought of myself as an author. But I started writing anyway – and thousands of readers have purchased my books. You might have a best-selling book in you too.

This next chapter will walk you through the process of writing your first book, starting with my top five reasons for self-publishing.

Five Reasons to Write a Book

1) Refine your ideas.

As you write and edit your book, you will spend hours figuring out the best way to explain your ideas. You'll develop metaphors and stories that illustrate your points. You'll think through the implications of your advice. You'll hone in on the core ideas you want to communicate.

And guess what? All that work will pay off during your therapy sessions. Instead of explaining a concept to a client off the top of your head, you'll teach them ideas that you've spent hours refining. Instead of using vague examples to illustrate your point, you'll be able to draw on the metaphors and stories you've developed for your book. Even if you never publish your book, you will still benefit from the time you spent writing.

2) Encourage clients to choose you

Most clients will comparison shop before choosing a therapist. Therapy is a big commitment, and clients understandably want the best therapist.

A book gives you a serious advantage during this comparison process. While other therapists might have similar credentials to you, you're probably the only one who has written a book. That makes you stand out.

If the client buys your book and enjoys what they read, you stand out even more. If a client finds your book helpful, they will probably conclude therapy with you will be helpful as well.

3) Create speaking opportunities

Speaking opportunities are a fantastic way to attract new clients.

Let's say you speak at a local PTA meeting about warning signs of adolescent depression. Parents listening to your talk are likely to send their depressed teenagers to you. Even if people in your audience aren't directly interested, they might remember you and tell their friends down the road.

You don't need a book to seek out speaking opportunities, of course. But a book makes it easier. After all, there are many therapists in the world, but not many therapist-authors. That extra credibility goes a long way towards convincing event organizers to sign you on as a speaker.

Plus, remember how writing a book helps you refine your ideas? Your presentation will be much better because you're sharing ideas you've developed over the course of months. And the better your presentation, the more likely you are to be invited back for more presentations.

Of course, this requires you to be a competent public speaker. You won't attract new clients if you go on stage and bomb your presentation. But public speaking can be learned.

The best option for learning public speaking is Toastmasters (Toastmasters.org). Toastmasters is an international organization that runs clubs where members can practice their public speaking skills. Your city probably has a Toastmasters club so sign up, and commit for 3-6 months of membership. I guarantee that you will be a competent speaker by the end of that time.

4) Make an impact

You probably became a therapist because you wanted to help people. A book provides a new way for you to do just that.

As a therapist, you have insights to offer that most people don't. You have years of graduate training and hundreds or thousands of hours of clinical experience. Ideas that seems second-nature to you could be a godsend to someone else.

If you take the time to write a quality book, it will be a conduit of that wisdom. Your readers will learn things from your book they might not learn anywhere else. And that matters. You might not see the impact your book makes, but your readers certainly will.

5) Earn more income

I put this one last because you probably won't make much money from your book. Sorry!

The average self-published book probably sells a few copies each month. If you get lucky, you might be able to sell a few each week. If you're unlucky, you might not sell any at all.

Of course, it's possible to sell a lot of copies. I sell several copies of my books every day, and plenty of other authors do as well.

But this is difficult to do, and takes a lot of effort. My sales are high because I work really hard at introducing new readers to my books. I spend hours each week marketing my books or responding to reader mail. I also have the advantage of a highly trafficked website (ImproveYourSocialSkills.com) which helps me attract readers.

I work hard to find offline opportunities to sell my books too. Many of my book sales come when I speak at a conference and sell books afterwards, or reach out to bookstores and ask to do a book signing. Some people suggest self-publishing a book as a way to build "passive" income, but trust me – there's nothing passive about getting your book in front of potential readers!

In other words, if you're willing to put a lot of work into marketing and promoting your book, and it's well-written, and you have some luck on your side.... then yes, you can earn some decent income from your book.

Otherwise, figure that your book is primarily a marketing tool for attracting new therapy clients. You'll still earn a little income, but it will just be a nice bonus, not a reason to write the book.

Your Book Writing Checklist

At this point, you might be considering starting your book. Here's what you need to do to make that book a reality.

Step 1: Test The Waters

Writing a book is a big commitment.

Writing will cost you many, many hours. Hiring an editor and cover designer will cost you hundreds of dollars. If you never finish your book, all that time and money is wasted.

So test the waters with a smaller challenge before you commit to writing a book. You wouldn't jump off a diving board without making sure you could swim first, right?

The best challenge to start with is the 30 day, 10 post challenge. It's based on a suggestion from marketing guru Seth Godin. Here's how it works:

1. Start a new blog somewhere, and don't put your name on it. This will give you the freedom to take risks without worrying about the consequences.

2. Write ten posts on this anonymous blog. Your posts can be about whatever you want. Experiment with different styles of posts, different topics, etc. If possible, write all ten posts within one month to maintain momentum.

3. After you've written ten posts, share a few with some trusted friends and get their feedback.

4. Then, decide what happens next. Do you feel ready to start writing a book? Do you want to continue writing for your blog? Do you want to give up on writing for the time being?

Writing this anonymous blog will teach you a lot. You might find that you enjoy writing and you're good at it. In that case, there's a decent chance you have a book in you!

Or, you might find that writing feels like a chore. Don't give up just yet!

Instead, put the blog on pause for a month or two, and read through one of the writing books that I'll mention in the next step. Then, give it another try. If it still doesn't work out for you, then probably writing a book isn't for you.

Step 2: Choose Your Topic

A reader takes a risk every time they buy a new book. Will they like the book, or will it be a waste of time and money? They're much more likely to take that risk if they have a clear sense of the value the book can offer them.

The easiest way to show the reader a clear sense of value is to pick a specific topic. If your book is organized around a specific topic, it's easy for readers to determine the value the book brings.

If you're not sure what topic you want to write on, here are two ideas.

Write about a specific condition

You might write a guide for a specific psychological condition, such as depression or anxiety.

There are already excellent guides written by experts for psychological disorders – but there's also a lot of junk out there. I just searched Amazon for "depression" and the third result was a book called "Depression: The Depression Cure: Cure Depression Instantly and Become Happy & More Confident Starting Today!"

Needless to say, this book was not written by an expert. Yet lots of people are buying it. If you published your own book on evidence-based depression advice and were able to take some sales away from charlatans claiming to "Cure Depression Instantly", you'd be doing the world a favor.

By the way, specific conditions don't have to be mental illnesses. You could easily write a book on better sleep habits, stress management skills, or effective study habits. Any problem that lots of people struggle with is a potential topic.

You can also take a positive psychology approach and write about a goal many people have instead of writing about a problem. For instance, you might write a psychological guide to running a marathon. Or you might write some therapeutic tips that people can use for better workplace performance.

If you decide to take this approach, start by thinking of goals you find personally meaningful. This will help you connect with your readers, and give you more insight to share.

Write for a specific population

Another option is to write a guide that helps a specific population with a specific issue.

For instance, let's say you work with a lot of geriatric patients, and you are skilled in treating depression. You could probably write a book of advice for elderly people who are depressed. Just take evidence-based advice for depression and combine it with examples and applications that are specific for the elderly.

The benefit of this approach is that you have much less competition. The more specific your topic, the fewer books there are written for it. There are many books written about depression in general, but very few written about geriatric depression. That makes it easier for your book to get noticed.

You also have a greater chance to make an impact. Someone searching for a general guide to managing their depression already have several excellent books they can choose from (as long as they can avoid the books peddling instant cures.) But your book may be the only good resource available for someone who needs help with elderly depression (or whatever topic you choose.)

If you're not sure what approach to take, I recommend writing for a specific population. It's the approach I took to this book – you'll notice I wrote about online marketing for therapists, not online marketing for everyone.

An easy way to start is to list the 3-4 populations you have the most experience with, and then the 3-4 conditions that you have the most skill in treating. Then do a quick Amazon search and see what material is already available for those conditions and those populations. If you find a niche that doesn't have many quality books, start brainstorming ideas for advice you could offer.

Step 3: Sit Down and Write the Darn Thing

Writing a book can be a bummer.

There's writer's block, of course. And the self-doubt that whispers, "You're a terrible writer – nobody will read this!" Even on days when your writing flows well and your confidence is high, there's no way around the long hours sitting at the keyboard.

But while writing a book is a bummer, having a book written is amazing. My life is profoundly better because I became an author. I think you'll also find writing a book is worth the sacrifice.

Of course, it takes more than sacrifice. You'll also need a writing strategy.

Some writers set aside a specific time every day to write. Other writers give themselves a specific quota of words to write every day. I find I work best in sprints – instead of writing a little every day, I set aside an entire evening to write once or twice a week. Experiment and see which strategy gets you the best results.

The good news is that there are a lot of resources for helping you to become a better (and more prolific) writer. My four favorites are:

- "The War of Art" by Stephen Pressfield
- "Bird by Bird" by Anne Lamott
- "On Writing Well" by William Zinsser
- "You Are a Writer" by Jeff Goins.

You can also find people to help you along the way. Many cities have writing groups that meet periodically (just check Meetup.com). You can also ask a friend to hold you accountable to your writing goals.

You might also try some software tools to help you write. I use FocusAtWill.com to – you guessed it! – help me focus. It's fantastic for helping me get into a flow. My sister wrote her dissertation in Scrivener (Literatureandlatte.com/scrivener.php) which has a lot of helpful book writing features. Feel free to experiment and find out what works for you.

Whatever support system you set up, make sure you commit to working on your book until it's done. There are a lot of would-be authors with unfinished books on their hard drive that will never be published. Don't be one of them.

Step 4: Edit, Edit, Edit.

If you want a book that people will enjoy reading, you need to invest a lot of time into editing it. So once you've finished your first draft, go back and edit.

Make your ideas as clear as possible. Make your writing flow smoothly. And for the love of Sigmund Freud, fix all your typos and grammar mistakes! Nothing kills your credibility faster than frequent typos.

The easiest way to edit your writing is to read it out loud. If it sounds awkward coming out of your mouth, it's probably awkward on the page too. Reading your writing out loud also forces you to slow down enough to notice grammar mistakes or other flaws in your writing.

You should also get others to help you during the editing stage. Asking friends to read your writing is a great option (as long as they know you want honest feedback, not compliments.) There are plenty of writing groups either in person or online where you can submit your writing for critique.

I recommend you also work with a professional editor. In general, you'll want to ask an editor to look at your first or second draft (to make sure you're on the right track) and then your final draft (to make sure everything is as polished as possible. You can ask for help throughout the process, of course, but first and last draft is usually the minimum to make sure you produce a quality book.

My suggestion for an editor and writing coach is my friend Tahlia Kirk (Tahliamkirk.com). She is the person I use for my own book editing, and she can help make your writing sparkle.

Step 5: Design Your Cover

You're not supposed to judge a book by its cover, but your readers definitely will.

The more professional your cover looks, the more credible you'll appear to potential clients. So the better your book cover, the more clients you attract and the more books you sell.

If you're a talented artist, you might try designing your own cover. However, most people will need to hire someone to help them.

I recommend Phillip Gessert (PhillipGessert.com). He designed the cover for this book and he does great work. As of April 2016, his fee for a custom book cover is $400.

At first glance, $400 might seem like a lot of money. But you get what pay for. Cheap book covers are usually made using stock photography and look generic and low-quality. While a low-quality book cover isn't the end of the world, it reflects poorly on your book content (and the book author – you!)

Of course, it's possible to find a cheap book cover that still looks great. If you want to try your luck, the best place to find cheap books covers is reddit.com/r/forhire. You'll get lots of up-and-coming designers looking for work, so you might find a talented newcomer who doesn't charge much yet. If you don't care about quality and just want the absolute cheapest cover you can get, try Fiverr.com – you can find covers for as low as $5.

Regardless of the designer you choose, make sure the cover looks good in small size. Amazon displays a tiny thumbnail version of book covers in the search results. If your book doesn't look good at small size, it's less likely that people will buy it.

Step 6: Publish Your Book!

Congratulations! Your book is written and edited, and you have a shiny new cover. Here's how to get your book into the hands of readers.

Kindle Direct Publishing

The first stop for self-publishing is Amazon Kindle. Amazon has a massive reach, lots of tools, and generous royalties. Most people have a Kindle (or at least the Kindle app), so Kindle is your best bet for reaching lots of readers.

Your first step is to sign up at kdp.amazon.com. Then, submit your book. There are a few stages to this:

Put in Your Book Details

You'll need to fill out the book title, description, etc. Most of this is pretty obvious (put your name in the "author" box, for instance), but there is one tricky part: The description.

Many novice authors write a sentence or two for their book's description. Don't fall into that trap. Write at least a few paragraphs and make a case for your book. Why would someone want to read it? Why are you qualified to write it? If you're not sure what to say, read the back covers of a few of your favorite non-fiction books for inspiration.

Also, use good formatting. If you clump everything together in one big paragraph, your description won't be very readable. Break your ideas up into small paragraphs and put spaces between your paragraphs. If your description doesn't look good once the book is published, go back and edit it (you can update your description as often as you want.)

Finally, make sure you choose good categories for your book to be listed in. Readers might discover your book by browsing the Amazon directory, so putting it in the right category makes it easier for it to be found. You'll also want to add some keywords to increase findability.

Set Pricing

You'll have to choose how much to charge for your Kindle book. Amazon pays you a better royalty (70% instead of 30%) when your book is priced between $2.99 and $9.99. So most of the time, you should choose to price your book in that range.

Here's a basic strategy for choosing your price:

- If you're not sure how much to charge, you should charge $2.99. That way, you get the 70% royalty, but it's still cheap enough to be an impulse purchase for most people.

- If you want to use your book primarily as a marketing tool and not as a source of income, price your book at 99 cents. You'll earn very little from each sale, but you'll maximize your readers – and hopefully some of those readers will become therapy clients.

- If your book is high quality and full length (100+ pages), you might charge $3.99 or $4.99. If you are going to charge this amount, you should plan to work hard marketing your book.

Also, Amazon will ask you if you want to sign up for KDP select. You should almost always say yes, because this gives you access to extra marketing tools (like running giveaways). The downside is that Kindle Unlimited subscribers can download your book for free, but the sales you lose from the free downloads is more than made up for by the benefits.

Format & Upload Your Book

You can upload a regular Word document to Kindle, but you need to make sure that it's formatted correctly. Search for "Formatting Book for Kindle" and you should find Amazon's official guide to making sure your book is formatted correctly. You can also hire a pro – the folks that I mentioned earlier (Phillip Gessert and Tahlia Kirk) are both able to format your document to make sure it looks great on Kindle.

Once you've uploaded your book, you should use Kindle's proofreading tool to make sure it all looks good. If you formatted the book yourself, you should go through page by page and check for errors. If you're hired a pro, just do a general once-over to make sure it all looks okay. If you find errors, fix them and resubmit.

You'll need to upload your cover as well, but this should be uneventful. Just make sure that your cover designer knows the right specifications for a Kindle cover.

Publish!

Once you hit publish, your book should be live on Kindle within a day or so. Congrats!

CreateSpace

If you want a physical copy of your book, you need to go through CreateSpace, which is also run by Amazon.

There are a lot of benefits to CreateSpace. They print your books on demand, which means it doesn't cost you anything to have your books listed. They also automatically distribute your books to Amazon, Barnes and Noble and other online booksellers, so you don't need to do anything to get your books in stores. And you can order copies of your own books for cheap, in case you want to give copies away or sell them at a conference or something.

You can sign up for free at CreateSpace.com. Once you publish your book through CreateSpace, it will automatically link itself to your Kindle book, so the two of them will appear together on Amazon.

Publishing a book through CreateSpace is a little more complicated than Kindle. Here are some of the differences:

- Your CreateSpace book cover needs to include the spine of the book as well as the back cover. Your cover designer should be able to handle this for you (although they might charge a little extra to make a CreateSpace version of your cover.) You also need to choose between a "glossy" and a "matte" cover – I use matte covers, but you can choose either.

- You will need to choose the size of the page. 6 x 9 is the most common, so choose that unless you have a good reason not to.

- You'll need to format your Word document to fit a printed book. Search for "CreateSpace formatting guide" and follow the steps. This is more complicated than formatting for Kin-

dle, so expect to invest a few hours. You can also hire someone like Tahlia or Phillip to do this for you.

• You will need to pick a price for your book. This price will
need to be higher than the ebook, because CreateSpace takes
a much higher royalty as a result of the costs in printing and
shipping the book. I recommend $9.99 unless you have a
good reason to go higher or lower.

Once your book is submitted to CreateSpace, you can order a "proof"
copy to make sure that everything looks good. Order your proof and
read through it once it arrives. If there are no errors, then you can put
your book on sale!

ACX

Acx allows you to produce an audiobook version of your book. It's also run by Amazon (see a theme here?), and automatically distributes
your book to Amazon, Audible, and iTunes. Since lots of folks prefer
audiobooks to reading, this expands your pool of potential book buy-
ers. You can sign up at Acx.com.

You'll need to hire a narrator to produce your audiobook. ACX has
an audition system where you can post your book and narrators all
around the world will record a short sample so you can gauge their
talent. Then you pick your preferred narrator and you are off and
running!

While ACX itself is free, you need to pay your narrator. ACX narrators
are paid in one of two ways.

First, you can agree on a royalty share plan. In this plan, the narrator
doesn't get paid anything up front, but they take 50% of the money
you earn from the audiobook – permanently. You should choose this
option if you're concerned your audiobook might sell poorly, or if you
just don't have enough money to pay a narrator up-front. Keep in
mind that not all narrators are willing to do royalty shares, so you
might not be able to use this option with your preferred narrator.

Otherwise, you can agree to pay the narrator a flat rate per finished
hour of audio. If your audiobook ends up being three hours long and
your narrator charges $200 per finished hour, you would pay them
$600. The rates that narrators charge can vary from $50 per finished

hour for narrators that are just starting out to $400+ for very experienced narrators.

I recommend Ryan Prizio (RyanPrizio.com) as a narrator. He has narrated all my audiobooks, he does excellent work, and his rates are pretty reasonable. If nothing else, I recommend you shoot him an email and invite him to audition – you can always choose someone else if you don't like the audition.

Step 7: Use Your Book to Promote Your Practice

Once your book is published, you should celebrate! But you're not quite done yet. Remember, you wrote the book as a marketing tool, so make sure you use it to market your practice.

The easiest way to do this is to feature the book prominently on your website. Ideally, you should put the book on your front page, although you might also include it in your menu. You might link people directly to the book's Amazon page, or you might offer them a free download of the first chapter in exchange for joining your mailing list.

You should also include a mention to your book in your online profiles. Update your social media accounts to include a link to the book, and if there is a biography of you on any professional sites (for instance, perhaps you are a professor at a local college) see if they can include a mention of the book. Again, your goal is to build credibility and increase the chances that someone might choose you as a therapist.

You can also use the book offline to build your practice. As I mentioned earlier, a book is a great way to convince event organizers to let you speak – and speaking gigs are great for building your practice. You might also consider seeing if the local newspaper is interested in interviewing your or running a story about your book, or if a local bookstore is willing to feature you for a book signing. All of these opportunities put you in front of potential clients – and help you sell some books too!

Oh, and consider giving some free copies to doctors, social workers, etc, and encourage them to give the books to the people they work with. This can backfire if you force books on people that don't want them, so ask before showing up with a crate of books!

These are not the only ways your book can help market your practice. Keep your eyes open for opportunities where your book might boost your credibility and increase your referrals. Good luck!

Profitable Online Advertising

Online advertising is a fantastic way to bring new clients to your website – or to lose a ton of money.

While sites like Yelp and Adwords Express promise to bring new clients without you lifting a finger, the truth is that successful online advertising requires a lot of work and a fair amount of expert knowledge.

The good news is that you've got an expert on your side – me! Before starting my graduate studies in psychology, I worked in online marketing for several years and managed millions of dollars in advertising for my clients. While I can't teach you everything I know, I can give you a head start. let's get started.

Online Advertising Crash Course

There's a reason I call this a crash course. I could easily write an entire book on online advertising and not tell you everything there is to know.

But a little knowledge goes a long way. Follow these tips, and you are much more likely to make a profit when advertising your practice.

Get a good website first

Online advertising generally sends visitors to your website. If your website is poorly designed, those visitors will leave and never come back.

So before you invest in online advertising, make sure your website is looking good. Spend the time to apply my advice on web design from earlier in the book, or hire the experts at BrighterVision.com to do it for you (mention my name to get a free month!)

Pick your platforms

You have a lot of options for advertising online.

- Search engines, like Google Adwords or Bing.
- Therapist directories, like Good Therapy and Psychology Today.
- Local directories, like Yelp and Yellowpages.com
- Social media like Facebook, Reddit and Twitter.

These different places to advertise are called "advertising platforms." It's important to pick the right platforms, because not all platforms will get you the same performance.

Here's some advice on choosing the right platform:

Directories

Good Therapy and Psychology Today are the most user friendly options for novice advertisers, but there's not much you can do to improve your performance beyond what I mention in my "therapist directories" section earlier in this book. I recommend trying them and seeing if they're profitable. If not, take your money elsewhere.

I haven't heard good things about local directories such as Yelp and Yellowpages.com, although you are welcome to test them and see what kind of results you get.

I wouldn't advertise on any directory you haven't heard of. If you haven't heard of it, clients probably haven't either. Save your money for the big-name directories.

Facebook

If you'd like to experiment with more advanced online advertising, try Facebook. Their advertising tool is fairly user friendly, but it's also powerful enough that you can learn the basics of online advertising strategy.

Bear in mind that it's easy to lose money on Facebook unless you target specific ads to specific groups. For instance, you might make an ad for a men's anger management group and target it only to men, and an ad for couple's counseling and target it only to married people.

Fair warning: plan to lose money at first. Facebook generally requires a lot of experimentation to find the right groups to target and the best way to reach them. While you might get lucky out of the gate, it's more likely that you'll need to do some trial-and-error before you become profitable. Start with low bids and low daily budgets to keep your costs under control while you experiment.

Google Adwords & Bing

Search engines such as Google or Bing are one of the best places to advertise, because you can reach people right when they're looking for therapy. Someone who searches for "couple's counseling" is definitely interested in couple's counseling. Someone who scrolls past your couple's counseling ad on Facebook might not be.

The problem is that search engines are very difficult to advertise on profitably. Although Google offers Adwords Express as a user-friendly option, Adwords Express usually doesn't get you very good results. The reason is that Adwords Express tends to show your ads to lots of people who are searching for something related to what you offer, but not actually what you offer. For instance, if you decide to advertise to people searching for therapy practices, Adwords Express might show your ad to someone who searches for the Private Practice TV show –potentially wasting your advertising dollars.

That's why I recommend that most therapists hire a professional if they want to advertise on Adwords or Bing. A professional is able to get you the best possible results and avoid the beginner mistakes that drain your advertising budget. I go into more detail on this in my section on Adwords later in the book, so read that if you want the full scoop.

Other Platforms

There are many other platforms that you can advertise on, such as Reddit, Twitter and Linkedin. You're welcome to experiment with them, but I think directories, Facebook and search engines are the platforms best suited for therapists.

If you do advertise on another platform, make sure it's a platform that allows you to geographically target your users within a small radius. Some platforms only allow you to target a specific country, which is not helpful at all (unless you happen to own a practice in a very small country!).

This is less of an issue if you offer online therapy, but online therapy has many ethical and practical challenges. If you're interested in pursuing this route, that must be overcome before you can offer it. I suspect most therapists stick to in-person therapy, which means using platforms that can target their local area.

Track your performance

Many therapists don't track the performance of their online advertising. If you're one of them, you could be wasting money every month without knowing it.

Even therapists that do track their results often track the wrong results. It's common for online advertising platforms to report metrics like likes, shares, and views. But you can't pay your bills with likes or shares. You need dollars for that, and your dollars come from clients.

So the metric you should pay attention to is called "Cost per acquisition" (CPA.) This metric measures the average amount you need to pay to get a new client. You calculate it by dividing the number of clients that an advertising platform has brought you by the amount you've spent on that platform. If you spent $500 on Adwords last month and brought in 5 clients, your Adwords CPA would be $100 (500/5).

Cost per acquisition determines the profit you earn from each new client. Let's say the average client comes to 8 sessions and pays you $100 per session. If you got a new client for free, then you would earn $800 in profit from that client. (For the sake of easy math, I am ignoring insurance and other variables, but make sure you factor them in. If you charge clients $100 but only receive $50 after insurance, use $50 to calculate your true profit per client.)

If your cost per acquisition is $100, then you earn $700 in profit from a new client. You're probably happy to earn $700 for 8 sessions of work, so this is a good CPA.

If your cost per acquisition is $700, then you only pocket $100 after working with the client for 8 sessions. That means you earned just $12.50 per hour – probably not worth your time.

And if your cost per acquisition is more than $800, then you are losing money on each new client!

So it's essential to track your cost per acquisition. That way, you know how much you are earning (or losing) from each new client that finds you through your ads.

The easiest way to track your CPA is to set up Google Analytics on your website. Then, set up conversion tracking within Google Analytics to record every time that someone fills out your contact form.

Setting up Google Analytics on your site and configuring conversion tracking sounds complicated, but it's not too bad. Just Google for "Google Analytics setup" and "Google Analytics conversion tracking" or ask your web person for help. If you're tech-savvy, you might also set up conversion tracking within the advertising platforms themselves (if not, don't worry about it.)

Once you've done this, you can see how many clients you received from your different advertising platforms. At the end of the month, take the number of clients you received from each advertising platform, divide it by the amount you spent on that platform and viola, you know what your CPA is for each platform.

Keep in mind that the results in Google Analytics are estimates. Google Analytics doesn't track the people who called you instead of filling out a contact form. It also measures the number of people who emailed you – but some people who email you might not end up coming in for therapy. So your actual cost per new client might be higher or lower than the cost per acquisition number you calculate. But even an estimate should help you make informed decisions.

Follow the money

Once you start tracking your performance, you can use that information to adjust your marketing budget.

If your cost per acquisition is highly profitable, you might consider spending more on advertising. If it's unprofitable, you might want to change your advertising strategy or hire a professional.

It's common for some platforms to be more profitable than others. Let's say Adwords brings you new clients at a $50 CPA and Facebook brings you new clients at a $125 CPA. That might be a sign that you should spend more money on Adwords and less on Facebook.

It might also mean you should rewrite your Facebook ads to improve performance. Or if you are satisfied with a $125 CPA, it might mean you should spend more money on both Adwords and Facebook.

There's no one-size-fits-all strategy; you need to consider your unique business needs when considering your results.

One final note: Performance does change over time. So check back every few months to stay up to date, and make the appropriate changes.

Bid wisely

Many online advertising platforms function on a bidding system. You choose the maximum amount you are willing to spend per click (or per view). The higher your bid, the more likely your ad shows instead of a competitor's.

Bidding strategy is complicated, and generally you need a professional to make the best possible bidding decisions. But there's a few things you can keep in mind to get started.

First, understand the relationship between traffic, cost per acquisition, and your bid. By raising your bid, you will increase your traffic, but you will also increase your cost per acquisition. So your goal is to raise your bid high enough that you get a lot of clients, but not so high that your cost per acquisition becomes unprofitable.

Second, your ads should have different bids based on their performance. If your couple's counseling ad is performing much better than your individual therapy ad, you probably want to raise the bids for your couple's counseling ad and lower the bids for your individual therapy ad.

Third, you should consider your advertising budget when choosing your bids. If you bid too low, you will get very little traffic and won't be able to spend your whole budget each day. If you bid too high, you will blow through your budget very quickly, and you will also get little traffic. It's best to bid just enough that your budget lasts all day and runs out towards the end. As a rule of thumb, if you are spending your entire budget every day, your bids are probably a little too high and you should consider lowering them. If you never spend your entire daily budget, your bids are probably too low and you should consider raising them.

Again, bidding strategy is complicated, and it's okay if you are confused at first. As you continue to experiment with online advertising, it will start to make more sense.

Research best practices

Before you decide to advertise on a new platform, do some research first. If you take the time to learn the best strategies and techniques for that platform, your ads are more likely to be profitable.

An easy way to generate a reading list is to go to Google and search for the following:

- [Name of Platform] advertising strategies
- [Name of Platform] advertising guide
- [Name of Platform] advertising best practices

You can also read through the guides in my "Recommended Resources" section later in this book.

Please don't skip this step. I know it seems tedious to spend hours reading about online advertising strategy. But if you don't take the time, how well do you think your ads will perform against competitors who have hired a professional? Give yourself a fighting chance and do your homework.

Know when to hire a professional

A professional marketer can significantly boost the performance of your online advertising. They can write more effective ads, target them to the right people, and make sure you are getting the most out of every advertising dollar.

Since professional marketers are expensive, you don't want to spend money without a good reason. So how do you know it's the right time to hire a professional?

Well, there's no perfect answer. But I'd say there are three situations when it makes a lot of sense:

1) *When your advertising budget is growing*

A professional multiplies the effect of your advertising budget. They might be able to get 50%, 100% or even 200% more clients than you could from the same advertising dollars. (The exact amount depends on the difference between your skill and theirs.)

The larger your advertising budget, the more this multiplier matters.

If your current budget is large enough to get you one client per month and a professional can double your performance, then hiring a pro will get you one extra client per month – not very much. If your current budget is large enough to get you 30 clients per month, then hiring a pro will get you 30 extra clients per month – quite a lot!

That's why the larger your budget grows, the more you should consider a professional. As a rule of thumb, you definitely don't need a professional if you are spending less than $100 per month, and you probably do need a professional if you're spending more than $1000.

2) *When your time is limited*

Running online advertising campaigns takes time. If you'd rather spend the time on other parts of your business (or your personal life), it might make sense to hire a professional.

Also, consider the stress factor. If online advertising causes your blood pressure to rise, it might be a form of self-care to let a professional handle your ads.

3) *When you're not sure what you're doing*

Online advertising is complicated, and it can be tricky to learn. That's why professionals are available to help.

As a general rule, you should hire a pro if you can't turn a profit even after a few months of trying. You should also hire a professional if you can't track your results well enough to determine if you're profitable.

If you are bound and determined to manage your own advertising but struggle to turn a profit, consider hiring a professional to teach you the ropes. Coaching can be expensive, but it often pays off over the long run. This is especially a good option if you don't have the time to do a lot of research and practice on your own.

Avoid unqualified professionals

Unlike therapists, online marketers are not required to become licensed. Pretty much anyone can declare themselves an online marketing guru, even if they have no clue what they're doing. Here are a few tips to make sure you find an actual expert:

1. Ask for references. Any qualified professional should be able to provide you with several happy customers you can contact.

2. Find out how they will track performance and measure success. If their answer only discusses "clicks" "impressions" "likes" or other non-revenue generating metrics, be very suspicious. A good answer should include the ways their work will make you more money.

3. Look for professionals with experience working for large clients. If a freelancer has successfully managed a client spending hundreds of thousands of dollars per year in online advertising, they can probably manage your account too. If a freelancer has only ever worked with mom and pop businesses, then be more suspicious. Unqualified people can still talk a small business into hiring them, but large businesses usually only hire experienced experts.

4. Be suspicious of large monthly management fees. Legitimate professionals will usually not charge more than 25% of your monthly ad spend to manage your account (so if you spend $1000 on advertising each month, they shouldn't charge more than $250 per month to manage it.) If they do have a large monthly management fee, ask them exactly what they are doing each month to justify that fee.

5. Conversely, be suspicious of very low fees. A legitimate online marketing expert should charge $100 per hour or more. If they're charging significantly less than that, triple-check their credentials. Remember that cutting costs by hiring a

poorly qualified "expert" will cost you more in wasted advertising dollars than it will save.

How to find qualified professionals

I could be biased, but I think the easiest way to make sure you are
working with an expert is to hire yours truly!

I have lots of references, a detailed explanation of how I track performance, more than four years of experience working for large clients,
and very reasonable management fees. I've also helped dozens of
therapists launch their accounts, and I'm training to be a therapist
myself (so I understand the industry!) If you're interested, get in
touch at marketingfortherapists.org/contact.

However, I want you to have all your options open. So if you want
to hire someone else, I recommend you make a "help wanted" post
in the forum at reddit.com/r/ppc. Lots of qualified professionals frequent that forum, and you should be able to find someone who can
help you.

I recommend against working with a marketing agency unless you
are planning on spending several thousand dollars on advertising
each month. Because marketing agencies have a lot of expenses (rent,
a sales team, etc), they need to earn a minimum amount of money
from each client. So they will either charge you a lot of money, or they
will give you very little service in order to cut their costs. Either way,
you lose.

Hire an individual freelancer instead. Freelancers have fewer expenses than agencies, so you are more likely to be an attractive client for
them. Of course, it's possible to find a good agency that will charge
you a fair amount – but in general, a freelancer is a safer bet.

Adwords Advertising for Therapists

My preferred platform for advertising is Google Adwords.

Adwords is Google's system for advertising in the Google search results.

Google shows an ad for your business in the search results and you pay when it gets clicked. For instance, you can create an ad that shows up when someone searches for "local therapist." If someone clicks on that ad, they go right to your website.

Why Do Therapists Need Adwords?

Adwords brings new clients to your therapy practice for an affordable price. I recommend it for almost any therapist.

Here's why:

The average client does about 9 sessions of therapy. Let's assume you charge $100 per session. At 9 sessions per client, that means a new client is worth $900 to you.

Adwords can bring you new client referrals for $100 or less. I know this because I run a lot of Adwords accounts for therapists, and I see these numbers in most of them.

If you spend $100 to land a client and they pay you $900, you've earned $800. That's a fantastic margin.

Best of all, you can track exactly how well Adwords is performing. You can see how much you're spending, and how much each new client referral is costing you. So there's no guesswork. You can know with certainty how successful Adwords is for you.

Why Hire an Adwords Expert?

Here's the catch:

The $100 per referral number I quoted you? You probably can't get that on your own.

Adwords is much like poker at the casino — anyone can play, but usually only the pros make money. There's a lot of strategy that goes into it, and if you don't know what you're doing, you'll lose money.

For instance, you pay for every single click you receive. So if someone searches for "physical therapist" and clicks on your ad, you've wasted money. So you need to set your ads to make sure they show up for someone searching for "therapist" and "mental health therapist" but not "physical therapist" — and this can be tricky to do.

Moreover, Adwords rewards effective advertisements. If your ad text gets clicked more than your competitors, Adwords gives you a discount. Similarly, if your ad text gets clicked less, you have to pay more. So one advertiser might pay $3 and one might pay $5 for the same click. Making sure your ads are as good as possible is another area where expertise helps a lot.

Also, Adwords has many features that a novice probably doesn't know how to use. You probably don't know the best strategies for things like structured snippets, dayparting and match types, but a professional does.

I could go on, but the point is pretty straightforward — you often get much better results from Adwords when you have a professional manage it.

Of course, I'm hoping you'll decide that professional will be me!

Why Work With Me?

I've been an Adwords consultant for over four years. It was my full-time job for three years, and I've continued working as a freelancer after entering my doctoral program in clinical psychology.

I was trained by some of the best minds in the business, and I've run everything from massive accounts spending over $100,000 per month to campaigns for small clients who wanted to spend their first $100. I understand Adwords inside and out, and as a graduate student in clinical psychology, I understand the world of therapy as well.

Plus, I'm passionate about this. If I can help a therapist grow their business, then they can see more clients, and more people get the help they need. That matters to me.

So I don't cut corners.

Some of my competitors make a big deal about creating four ad groups and dozens of keywords. I give you over a hundred of each.

I also talk with each client to figure out what makes them unique as a therapist, and use that information to craft custom ads and keywords.

The bottom line?

When I say you're in good hands with me — trust me, you're in good hands

What I Offer

If you hire me to set up your account, here's what you get:

Adwords Setup Package

- 100+ highly relevant keywords, customized to your areas of specialty.
- 100+ tightly organized ad groups
- 2 ads per ad group, set to compete and choose a winner
- Customized ad text and hand-picked destination URLs
- Expert configuration of all campaign settings and ad extensions
- Help with setting up conversion tracking.

- 3 months of management and optimization (described below)

- 3 months of reports, describing account performance and insights for your business (described below)

- The satisfaction of knowing you are helping put me through grad school

Testimonials

Dan is a great guy and the real deal. He's genuine, approachable, and knows how to optimize paid advertising for therapists.

-Joe Sanok, MA, LLP, LPC, NCC, PracticeOfThePractice.com

Daniel Wendler knows his stuff. He has helped so many people get their private practice marketing moving like a well-oiled machine, and his warm, engaging personality makes him a pleasure to work with.

-Jane Carter, LPC, President of the National Association of Counselors in Private Practice, PrivatePracticeCounselors.com

I couldn't be more pleased with Dan's work! He has essentially taken his vast knowledge and formidable skill set and applied it to my practice as if it were his own. I unhesitatingly recommend him.

-Mike Pecosh, M.Ed., NCC, LPC, WashingtonTherapist.com

Whenever a client is looking to grow their practice through Adwords, we always refer them to Dan. He consistently goes above and beyond for our clients and we view him as the best Adwords expert in the industry for therapists.

-Perry Rosenbloom, CEO, BrighterVision.com

FAQ

Got questions? I've got answers.

How much should I spend on Adwords each month?

I normally recommend therapists plan to spend $500 per month on Adwords. That gives you 100 – 200 clicks per month, which is a pretty good number.

Of course, you can spend less, but it will take longer for you to see results. You can also spend more than this amount if you want to grow your practice even faster. But I find that most therapists are satisfied with the traffic they get for $500 per month.

How much do you charge?

You can see my current rates at Marketingfortherapists.org/adwords-for-therapists. I also offer discounts to recent grads or nonprofits.

What is the difference between Adwords and SEO?

Google's search results are a combination of ads (placed there by advertisers) and what are called "organic" results (placed there by Google's algorithm.) Adwords is the system you use to manage your advertisements, while SEO refers to the techniques you use to convince Google's algorithm that your site deserves to show up in the free listings.

Or to put it another way –Adwords is like paying the bouncer at a club the cover fee every time you want to enter. SEO is like trying to convince the bouncer that you are a celebrity and he should let you in for free.

Should I invest in Adwords or SEO?

In a perfect world, you'd invest in both. But if you have a limited budget, I recommend starting with Adwords.

While both Adwords and SEO can help you bring in traffic, SEO takes longer and requires more work. With Adwords, you're competing against the handful of other therapists who are also using Adwords. With SEO, you're competing against every single local therapist with a website. That means it can take months before your efforts start to pay off.

That's why most therapists should start with Adwords. Adwords brings you traffic immediately, and allows you to start seeing new clients right away. Of course, if you can invest in both SEO and Adwords, go for it. But since Adwords has the quicker payoff, I usually recommend that people start there, and use some of the profits from Adwords to invest in their SEO strategy.

How do I sign up?

Just go to MarketingForTherapists.org/Contact and let me know you're interested!

Recommended Resources

You've reached the end of the book – congratulations! (Unless you skipped straight here in – in which case go back and read the book!)

As a way of saying thank you for reading my book, I've compiled a list of my favorite resources. Enjoy!

My Recommendations

Helpful private practice websites

Marketing for Therapists (MarketingForTherapists.org) – My website! If you want to hire me to help with your marketing, or if you just have questions, this is the place to go.

Practice of The Practice (PracticeOfThePractice.com) – Joe Sanok's guide to running a successful therapy practice. His site is full of free advice, and he runs my favorite podcast on private practice success. He's also available for one on one coaching if you want to take your practice to the next level.

ZynnyMe (Zynnyme.com) – Run by a pair of successful therapists, Zynnyme offers a lot of free trainings on topics like setting the right fee for your practice or finding new streams of income. Like Practice of the Practice, you can also sign up for coaching with the ZynnyMe team.

National Association of Counselors in Private Practice (PrivatePracticeCounselors.com) – The NACPP has a variety of helpful articles and links on their website. Their blog is frequently updated, so it's a good way to keep on top of the latest news in the world of private practice.

Brighter Vision (BrighterVision.com) – Brighter Vision makes custom websites for therapists. If you want a beautiful website, give them a call. Mention my name to get your first month free.

Helpful online marketing guides

The Moz Guide to SEO (Moz.com/beginners-guide-to-seo) – Moz is one of the leading names in SEO. If you want a deep explanation of search engine optimization, this is the place to go.

Search Engine Land's Guide to SEO (Searchengineland.com/guide/seo). Another helpful guide to SEO. Between this and Moz, you should feel prepared to boost your rank in the search results.

Wordstream PPC U (Wordstream.com/learn) – A fantastic beginner's guide to pay-per-click advertising, including Facebook and Adwords. Required reading before you start advertising online.

Copywriting 101 (Copyblogger.com/copywriting-101) - Copyblogger is one of the best sites for learning how to write for the web. Their free Copywriting 101 course will take you through everything you need to know to be an effective online writer. If you want more Copyblogger goodness, check out the rest of their guides at Copyblogger.com/Learn.

Kissmetrics Marketing Guides (Blog.Kissmetrics.com/marketing-guides) – A wide variety of online marketing guides. This is a great place to go for information on less commonly used advertising platforms, such as Tumblr or Reddit.

Google Primer (YourPrimer.com) – Google Primer is a free app that gives you quick lessons on online marketing. Sneak in a lesson whenever you have five minutes of free time.

Adespresso Academy (Adespresso.com/academy/guides). Free guides to Facebook advertising for both beginner and intermediate advertisers. Start with their beginner's guide (Adespresso.com/academy/guides/facebook-ads-beginner).

Helpful people

Kyler Shumway (WritingforTherapists.org). Kyler is a good friend of mine and an excellent ghostwriter. If you need content for your website or blog, he can write it for you. Since he is currently training to be a psychologist alongside me, he is very knowledgeable about therapy and can write accurate content for your site.

Phillip Gessert (Phillipgessert.com) - I discovered Phillip when I was working on my previous book *Level Up Your Social Life*. Phillip designed a fantastic cover for me, and also formatted the interior of my book. If you are writing an ebook or if you need other graphic design help (like a logo), you should absolutely get in contact with Phillip.

Tahlia Kirk (Tahliamkirk.com) - Tahlia is another friend of mine and a skilled editor. If you need an editor or a writing coach, she's the first person you should call.

Ryan Prizio (Ryanprizio.com) - Ryan is the narrator for all my audiobooks. He does great work and is a consummate professional. If you are interested in producing an audiobook, Ryan is your guy.

Miscellaneous helpful websites

Focus @ Will (Focusatwill.com) - Focusatwill plays music that helps you focus. Most of this book was written with Focusatwill playing in the background, and I can testify that it works. It's a great tool for boosting your productivity (especially if you struggle with writer's block or procrastination)

Todoist (Todoist.com) – The best to-do list that I've found. It's accessible on all your devices and is super user friendly. Use it to keep track of your marketing goals or anything else you want to accomplish!

Vistaprint (Vistaprint.com) - If you don't have business cards, go here. You never know when they might come in handy, and having a professional card builds your credibility. Pay a little bit extra and get high quality cards.

MailChimp (Mailchimp.com) – I don't cover email marketing in this guide because – like social media – it doesn't tend to be a good investment of time for most therapists. But if you'd like to try writing a newsletter, use Mailchimp. It's free for up to 2,000 newsletter subscribers, and it's easy to use. Kissmetrics (linked above) has a good guide to email marketing which you should read if you decide to try Mailchimp.

Improve Your Social Skills (ImproveYourSocialSkills.com) - My first (and most popular) website. Helpful if you want to build your confidence for things like public speaking or book signings. You might also find content to share with your clients.

About the Author

I'm Dan, and I like people.

A few things about me:

- I left my career in online marketing to pursue a doctorate in clinical psychology in Portland, Oregon. So far the change has been totally worth it.

- This is my third book. I'm also the author of "Improve Your Social Skills" and "Level Up Your Social Life: The Gamer's Guide To Social Success" (as well as ImproveYourSocial-Skills.com). Both books are available on Amazon.

- I spoke at TEDx about "My Life With Asperger's." If you'd like to learn more about my personal story, you can watch my talk at http://bit.ly/tedxdan.

Thanks again for reading the book! If you found it helpful, do me a favor and leave a review on Amazon (or share it with your friends!)

If you have any questions or comments for me, feel free to get in touch at MarketingforTherapists.org/Contact.

And if you are interested in working together, I'd love to help. Shoot me an email and let's start growing your practice together!

Made in the USA
Las Vegas, NV
18 December 2021

38595324R00066